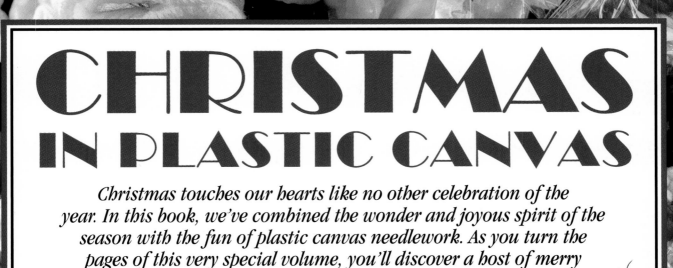

CHRISTMAS
IN PLASTIC CANVAS

*Christmas touches our hearts like no other celebration of the
year. In this book, we've combined the wonder and joyous spirit of the
season with the fun of plastic canvas needlework. As you turn the
pages of this very special volume, you'll discover a host of merry
projects — from colorful tree ornaments to holiday accents
for the home. Have a magical celebration!*

Eleanor

LEISURE ARTS, INC.
and
OXMOOR HOUSE, INC.

CHRISTMAS IN PLASTIC CANVAS

EDITORIAL STAFF

Vice President and Editor-in-Chief:
Anne Van Wagner Childs
Executive Director: Sandra Graham Case
Executive Editor: Susan Frantz Wiles
Publications Director: Carla Bentley
Creative Art Director: Gloria Bearden
Production Art Director: Melinda Stout

PRODUCTION
Managing Editor: Teal Lee Elliott
Project Coordinators: Michelle Goodrich, Catherine Hubmann, Susan McManus Johnson, and Rhonda Goerke Lombardo

EDITORIAL
Senior Editor: Linda L. Trimble
Senior Editorial Writer: Laurie S. Rodwell
Associate Editor: Dorothy Latimer Johnson

ART
Crafts Art Director: Rhonda Hodge Shelby
Production Artists: M. Katherine Yancey, Kenny L. Gipson, Sonya Cates, Karen L. Wilson, Roberta Aulwes, Katie Murphy, and Susan Gray Vandiver
Creative Art Assistant: Judith Howington Merritt
Photography Stylists: Lynn Loehle Bell, Sondra Harrison Daniel, Karen Smart Hall, Rhonda H. Hestir, Charlisa Erwin Parker, and Christy Tiano
Typesetters: Cindy Lumpkin and Stephanie Cordero

BUSINESS STAFF

Publisher: Bruce Akin
Vice President, Finance: Tom Siebenmorgen
Vice President, Retail Sales: Thomas L. Carlisle
Retail Sales Director: Richard Tignor
Vice President, Retail Marketing: Pam Stebbins
Retail Customer Services Director: Margaret Sweetin
General Merchandise Manager: Russ Barnett

Distribution Director: Ed M. Strackbein
Executive Director of Marketing and Circulation:
Guy A. Crossley
Circulation Manager: Byron L. Taylor
Print Production Manager: Laura Lockhart
Print Production Coordinator: Nancy Reddick Baker

CHRISTMAS IN PLASTIC CANVAS
from the *Plastic Canvas Creations* series
Published by Leisure Arts, Inc., and Oxmoor House, Inc.

Hardcover ISBN 0-8487-4125-0
Softcover ISBN 1-57486-037-2

TABLE OF CONTENTS

THE TWELVE DAYS OF CHRISTMAS

Images from "The Twelve Days of Christmas" are captured in rich, gleaming colors on these beaded ornaments. Created on 14 mesh canvas and finished with gold metallic ribbon, the lovely trimmings add elegance to a simple tree.

Skill Level: Intermediate

Size: 3"w x 3"h each

Supplies: Two 8⅛"x 10⅞" sheets of 14 mesh plastic canvas, #10 crewel needle, #24 tapestry needle, Mill Hill® Glass Seed Beads (refer to color keys), Kreinik ¹⁄₁₆" w metallic gold ribbon, and white quilting thread

Stitches Used: Beaded Tent Stitch and Overcast Stitch

Instructions: Follow chart and use required stitches to work Ornament. Use metallic gold ribbon Overcast Stitches to cover unworked edges of Ornament. For hanger cut a 2" length of metallic gold ribbon. Fold ribbon in half and secure ends on wrong side of stitched piece.

- 00081 jet
- 00123 cream
- 00148 pale peach
- 00150 grey
- 00332 emerald
- 00557 old gold
- 02015 sea blue
- 02023 root beer

- 00081 jet
- 00123 cream
- 00150 grey
- 00332 emerald
- 00367 garnet
- 00557 old gold

Designed by Carol Krob.

Partridge (41 x 41 threads)

Turtle Dove (41 x 41 threads)

French Hens (41 x 41 threads)

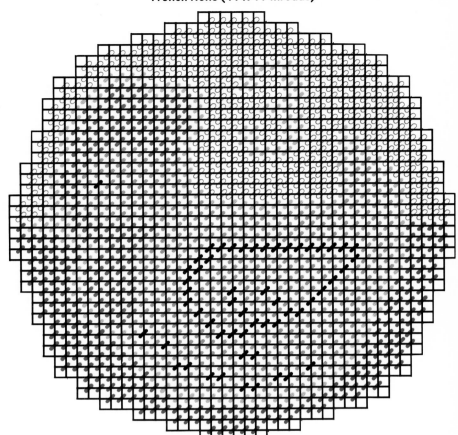

Calling Birds (41 x 41 threads)

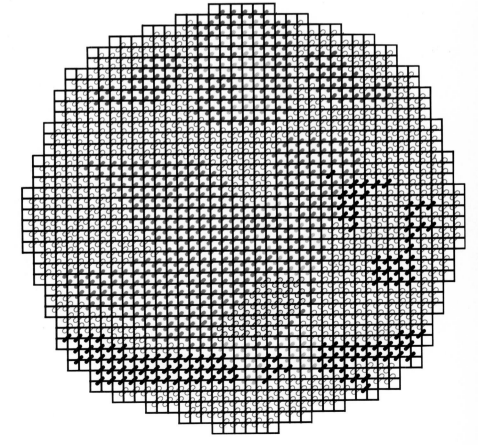

Gold Rings (41 x 41 threads)

00123 cream
00332 emerald
00367 garnet
00557 old gold

Geese-a-Laying (41 x 41 threads)

00081 jet
00123 cream
00332 emerald
00367 garnet
00557 old gold

Swans-a-Swimming (41 x 41 threads)

- ☑ 00081 jet
- ☑ 00123 cream
- ☑ 00150 grey
- ☑ 00358 cobalt blue
- ☑ 00367 garnet
- ☑ 00557 old gold

Maids-a-Milking (41 x 41 threads)

- ☑ 00081 jet
- ☑ 00123 cream
- ☑ 00148 pale peach
- ☑ 00275 coral
- ☑ 00332 emerald
- ☑ 00358 cobalt blue
- ☑ 00367 garnet
- ☑ 00557 old gold
- ☑ 02015 sea blue
- ☑ 02023 root beer

Drummers Drumming (41 x 41 threads)

- ✏ 00123 cream
- ✏ 00332 emerald
- ▧ 00367 garnet
- ✏ 00557 old gold
- ✏ 02023 root beer

Pipers Piping (41 x 41 threads)

- ✏ 00081 jet
- ✏ 00123 cream
- ✏ 00332 emerald
- ▧ 00367 garnet
- ✏ 00557 old gold
- ✏ 02023 root beer

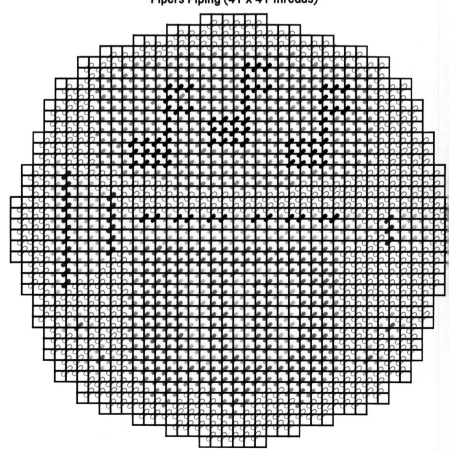

Ladies Dancing (41 x 41 threads)

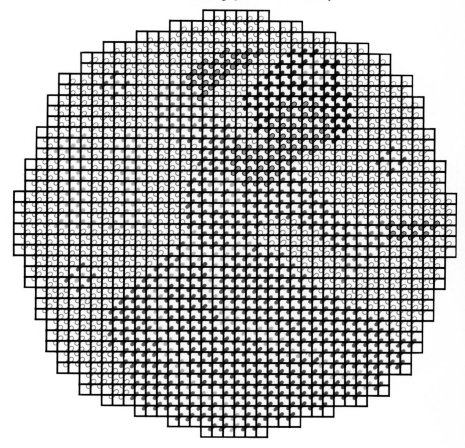

- ☑ 00123 cream
- ☑ 00275 coral
- ☑ 00332 emerald
- ☑ 00358 cobalt blue
- ☑ 00367 garnet
- ☑ 00557 old gold
- ☑ 02015 sea blue
- ☑ 02023 root beer

Lords-a-Leaping (41 x 41 threads)

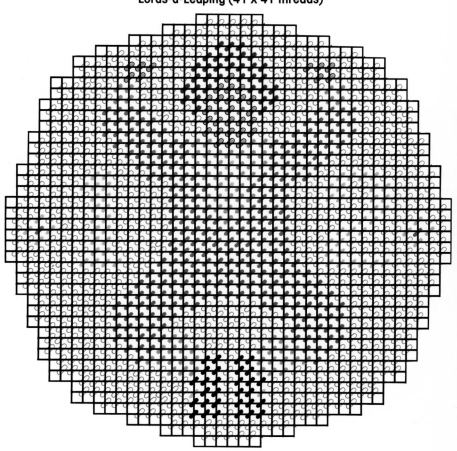

- ☑ 00081 jet
- ☑ 00123 cream
- ☑ 00275 coral
- ☑ 00332 emerald
- ☑ 00358 cobalt blue
- ☑ 00367 garnet
- ☑ 00557 old gold
- ☑ 02015 sea blue
- ☑ 02023 root beer

Cheery Christmas Ensemble

From the glowing candles on the boutique tissue box cover to the Yuletide motifs on the coordinating coasters and tree ornaments, this holiday ensemble is bursting with Christmas cheer! The matching door hanger, trimmed with shiny bells and a satin bow, announces visitors with a merry jingle.

Stitches Use~
Gobelin Sti~
Stitch

TISSUE~
Size: ~
(Not~
boun~
Instruction~
required stitch~
pieces. Use white f~
along long edges. Join t~

DOOR SIGN
Size: 5"w x 10⅝"h
Instructions: Follow chart and use required stitches to work Door Sign. Thread ribbon through bottom center of Door Sign and jingle bells, tie in bow and trim ends.

COASTERS
Size: 4"w x 4"h each
Instructions: Follow chart and use required stitches to work Coaster. If backing is desired, cut cork or felt slightly smaller than Coaster and glue to wrong side of stitched piece.

ORNAMENTS
Size: 3"w x 3"h each
Instructions: Follow chart and use required stitches to work Ornament. Cut an 8" length of nylon line. Thread nylon line through top center of Ornament. Knot ends of nylon line together 3" above top of Ornament.

◨ white

◨ green

Ornament #1 (21 x 21 threads)

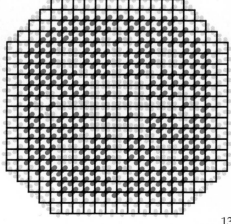

Skill Level: Beginner

Supplies: Worsted weight yarn (refer to color keys), three 10⅝" x 13⅝" sheets of 7 mesh plastic canvas, #16 tapestry needle, nylon line, #26 tapestry needle (for working with nylon line), cork or felt (optional), two 15mm gold jingle bells, 12" of ⅛"w green satin ribbon, Kreinik ⅛"w metallic gold ribbon, and clear-drying craft glue

✎ red - 90 yds

✎ green - 30 yds

✎ grey - 15 yds

✎ metallic gold ribbon - 15 yds

✎ yellow/lt green *

* Use 2 plies of each color.

Tissue Box Cover Top (31 x 31 threads)

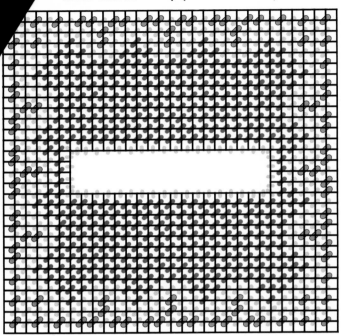

Tissue Box Cover Side (31 x 39 threads) (Work 4)

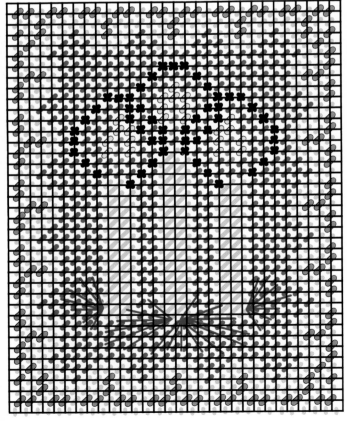

Door Sign (33 x 71 threads)

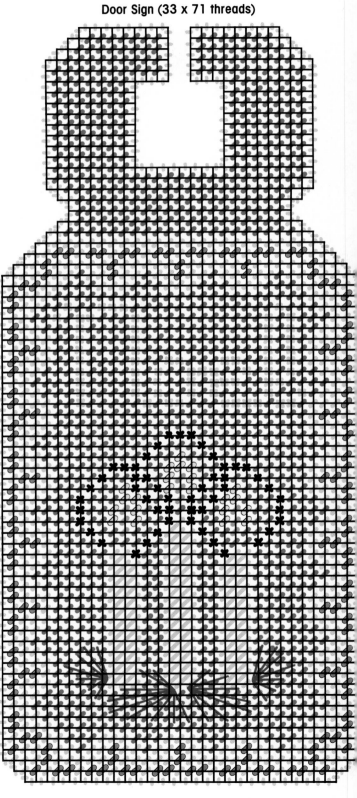

Designed by Jack Peatman for LuvLee Designs.

Coaster #1 (27 x 27 threads)

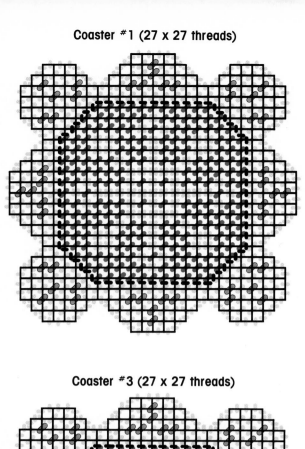

Coaster #2 (27 x 27 threads)

Coaster #3 (27 x 27 threads)

Coaster #4 (27 x 27 threads)

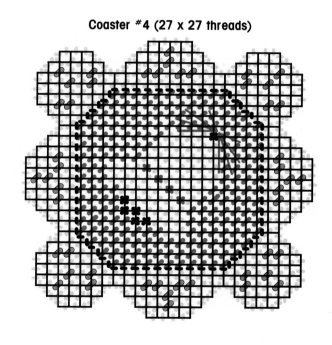

Ornament #2 (21 x 21 threads)

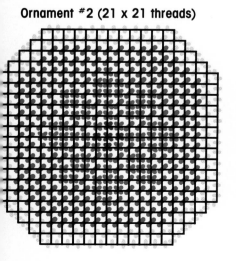

Ornament #3 (21 x 21 threads)

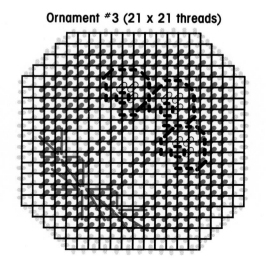

Ornament #4 (21 x 21 threads)

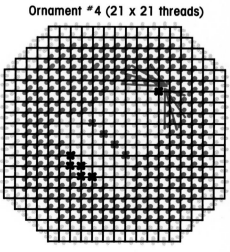

15

Holy Night Wall Hanging

The joy of the Saviour's birth shines brightly in this striking holiday wall hanging. The colorful piece is stitched on 10 mesh canvas with embroidery floss to create the beautiful look of stained glass.

Skill Level: Intermediate

Size: 14½"w x 12"h

Supplies: DMC embroidery floss (refer to color keys), one 10⅝" x 13⅝" sheet of 10 mesh plastic canvas, #20 tapestry needle, four 4" lengths of 1"w black satin ribbon, 13" length of ⅜" dia wooden dowel (may be painted), two end caps or beads (may be painted), two 18" lengths of cord with tassels on each end, and clear-drying craft glue or hot glue gun and glue sticks

Stitches Used: Gobelin Stitch, Overcast Stitch, and Tent Stitch

Instructions: Cut a piece of plastic canvas 109 x 109 threads. Follow charts and use required stitches to work sections, using 12 strands of embroidery floss for all stitches. Refer to Diagram for section placement. Use black Overcast Stitches to cover unworked edges. Refer to photo to glue ends of ribbons to wrong side of stitched piece, forming loops. Thread dowel through loops. Glue end caps to dowel. Refer to photo to tie each cord into a bow around dowel.

Designed by Mary Billeaudeau.

✎	310 black
✎	321 red
✎	400 brown
✎	666 lt red
✎	676 lt gold
✎	699 green
✎	712 off white
✎	725 yellow
✎	781 dk gold
✎	783 gold
✎	798 blue
✎	986 lt green
✎	3325 lt blue

Section 1

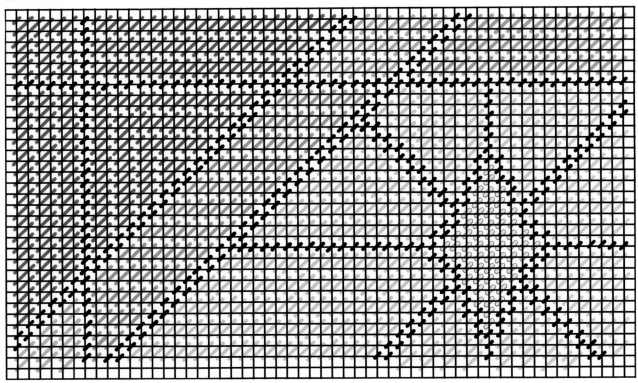

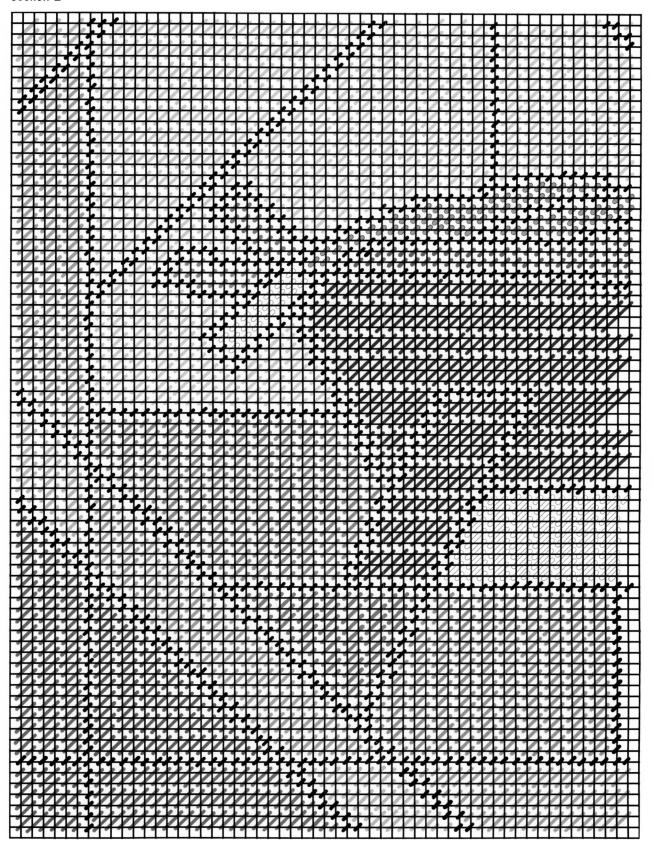

	310 black (6)
	321 red (2)
	400 brown (2)
	666 lt red (1)
	676 lt gold (1)
	699 green (2)
	712 off white (1)
	725 yellow (1)
	781 dk gold (2)
	783 gold (1)
	798 blue (6)
	945 flesh (1)
	986 lt green (3)
	3325 lt blue (1)

1	3
2	4

The number in parentheses after color name represents the number of skeins of embroidery floss needed to complete project.

Section 3

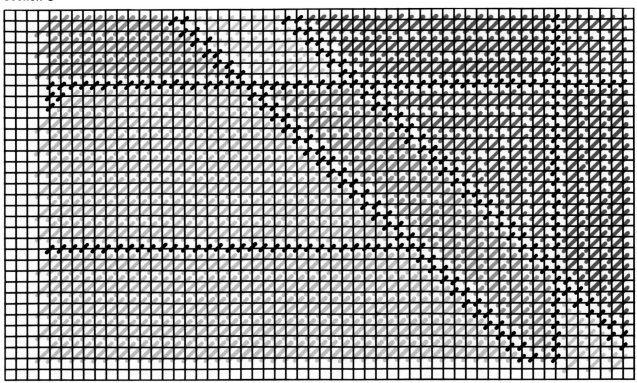

Pretty Poinsettia Coasters

Pretty poinsettia-shaped coasters will protect your tabletops in festive style! Also known as the Flower of the Holy Night, the brilliant blossoms will add an extra splash of color to your holiday entertaining.

Coaster (30 x 30 threads) (Work 4)

Skill Level: Beginner

Size: 4½"w x 4½"h

Supplies: Worsted weight yarn (refer to color key), one 10⅝" x 13⅝" sheet of 7 mesh plastic canvas, #16 tapestry needle, cork or felt (optional), and clear-drying craft glue

Stitches Used: Backstitch, French Knot, Overcast Stitch, and Tent Stitch

Instructions: Follow chart and use required stitches to work Coaster. If backing is desired, cut cork or felt slightly smaller than Coaster and glue to wrong side of stitched piece.

Designed by Jack Peatman for LuvLee Designs.

- ▨ red - 7 yds
- ◩ dk red 2-ply - 1 yd
- ▨ green - 3 yds
- ⦿ yellow/green Fr. Knot -1 yd*

*Use 2 plies of each color.

SPECIAL DELIVERY

Santa Claus is coming your way with a special delivery! Perfect for display indoors or out, this merry door decoration features a pouch to hold Christmas cards and other holiday mail. The textured "fur" trim on the jolly gentleman's familiar red suit is created with turkey loop stitches.

Skill Level: Advanced
Size: 10"w x 20¼"h
Supplies: Worsted weight yarn (refer to color keys), three 10⅝" x 13⅝" sheets of 7 mesh plastic canvas, #16 tapestry needle, sawtooth hanger, sewing needle, and thread
Stitches Used: Alternating Scotch Stitch, Cross Stitch, Gobelin Stitch, Overcast Stitch, Tent Stitch, and Turkey Loop

Instructions: Follow charts and use required stitches to work pieces, leaving shaded area unworked. Match ▲'s and work stitches in shaded area through two thicknesses to join Section A to Section B. Use brown and match ◒'s to join Right Hand to Santa. Use brown and match ■'s to join Left Hand to Santa. Use green to join Pouch Sides to Pouch Bottom along short edges. Use green to join Pouch Front to Pouch Sides and Pouch Bottom. Use green and match x's to join Pouch to Santa. Use brown and match ♦'s to join Hands to Pouch Front. Refer to photo and use white to tack Mustache to Santa. For hanger, sew sawtooth hanger to wrong side of stitched piece.

Designed by Jack Peatman for LuvLee Designs.

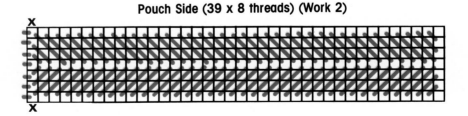

Pouch Side (39 x 8 threads) (Work 2)

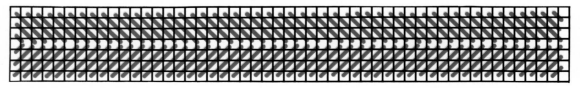

Pouch Bottom (52 x 8 threads)

◪ white
◪ red
◪ green - 5 yds
◪ dk green - 16 yds
◪ brown - 10 yds

Right Hand (19 x 18 threads)

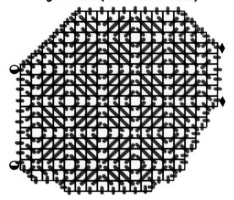

Left Hand (19 x 18 threads)

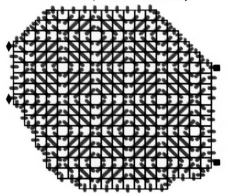

Pouch Front (48 x 44 threads)

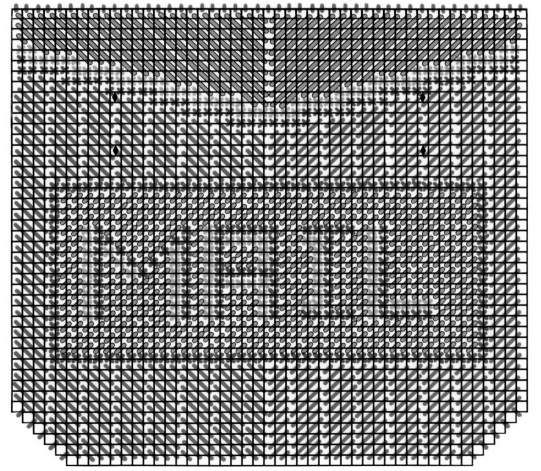

 white - 60 yds	
 peach - 3 yds	
pink - 2 yds	
red - 50 yds	
dk red - 5 yds	
blue - 1 yd	
grey - 4 yds	
black - 23 yds	
white Turkey Loop	

white - 60 yds
peach - 3 yds
pink - 2 yds
red - 50 yds
dk red - 5 yds
blue - 1 yd
grey - 4 yds
black - 23 yds
white Turkey Loop

Mustache (22 x 6 threads)

Section B (66 x 59 threads)

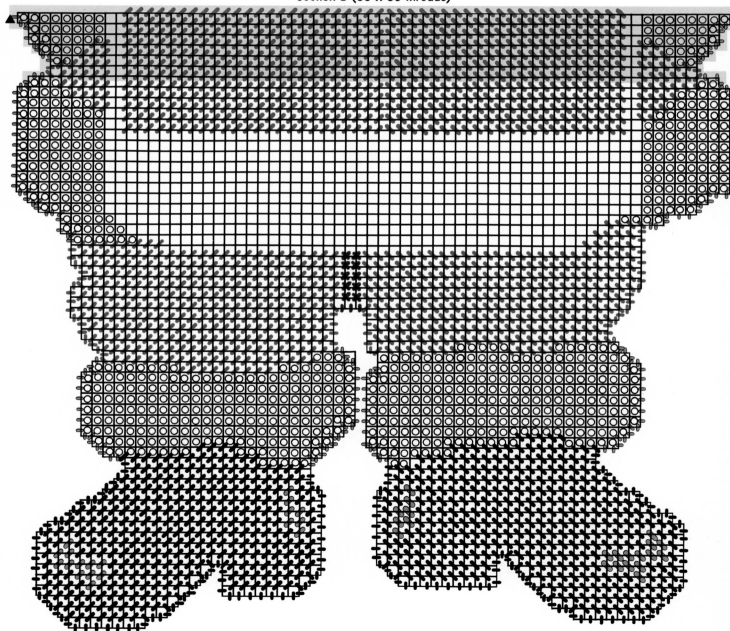

Section A (66 x 82 threads)

CHRISTMAS CANDY

These candy ornaments look good enough to eat! From lollipops to pinwheel peppermints, all your favorite Christmas treats can be found on this delicious-looking tree. Available in five ''flavorful'' designs, the decorations are quick and easy to make for yourself or to share with friends.

Skill Level: Intermediate

Supplies: Worsted weight yarn (refer to color key), one 10⅝" x 13⅝" sheet of 7 mesh plastic canvas, #16 tapestry needle, nylon line, #24 tapestry needle (for working with nylon line), 4" long lollipop sticks, white sewing thread, clear cellophane, and clear-drying craft glue

Stitches Used: Cross Stitch, Gobelin Stitch, Overcast Stitch, and Tent Stitch

TREE NOUGAT CANDY

Size: 2¼"w x 2¼"h x ½"d

Instructions: Follow charts and use required stitches to work Tree Nougat pieces, leaving stitches in shaded areas unworked. Match ✳'s and work stitches in shaded areas through two thicknesses to join ends of Tree Nougat Side. Use red to join Tree Nougat Front and Tree Nougat Back to Tree Nougat Side. For wrapper, cut an 8" square of cellophane. Refer to photo to wrap cellophane around Tree Nougat Candy. Use sewing thread to tie cellophane in place. For hanger, tie an 8" length of nylon line around top of wrapper. Tie ends of nylon line together in a knot.

CANDY CANE

Size: 1⅝"w x 3¼"h

Instructions: Follow charts and use required stitches to work Candy Cane pieces. With wrong sides together, use color to match stitching area to join Candy Cane Side A to Candy Cane Side B along unworked edges. For hanger, thread an 8" length of nylon line through top of Candy Cane and tie ends together in a knot 3" above ornament.

LOLLIPOP

Approx Size: 2⅞"w x 7½"h

Instructions: Follow chart and use required stitches to work Lollipop pieces. Refer to photo to glue a lollipop stick to the wrong side of Lollipop Back between ▲'s. With wrong sides together, use candy color and match ▲'s to join Front to Back along unworked edges. For wrapper, cut an 8" square of cellophane. Refer to photo to wrap cellophane around Lollipop. Use sewing thread to tie cellophane in place. For hanger, tie an 8" length of nylon line around top of wrapper. Tie ends of nylon line together in a knot.

PEPPERMINT

Approx Size: 2¼"w x 6½"h x ½"d

Instructions: Follow charts and use required stitches to work Peppermint pieces, leaving stitches in shaded areas unworked. Match ✳'s and work stitches in shaded areas through two thicknesses to join ends of Peppermint Side. Use color to match stitching area to join Peppermint Front and Peppermint Back to Peppermint Side. For wrapper, cut an 8" square of cellophane. Refer to photo to wrap cellophane around Peppermint. Use sewing thread to tie cellophane in place. For hanger, tie an 8" length of nylon line around top of wrapper. Tie ends of nylon line together in a knot.

Peppermint designed by Vicky Faber.

▨	white
▨	red
▨	green
▨	brown
▨	candy color

Tree Nougat Front/Back
(15 x 15 threads) (Work 2)

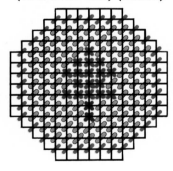

Peppermint Front/Back
(15 x 15 threads) (Work 2)

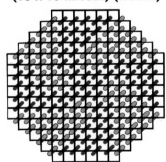

Peppermint Side
(49 x 3 threads)

Tree Nougat Side
(49 x 3 threads)

RIBBON CANDY

Approx Size: 1½"w x 1½"h x 1"d

Instructions: Follow charts and use required stitches to work unshaded areas. Turn plastic canvas strip over. Follow chart and use required stitches to work shaded areas. Refer to **Fig A** to bend plastic canvas strip. (**Note:** When plastic canvas strip is properly positioned, only the right side of stitching will show). Thread needle with an 18" length of candy color yarn. Starting at one end of folded strip, insert needle through all thicknesses of canvas at ♦'s. With same yarn, insert needle through all thicknesses of canvas at ◓'s. Gently pull yarn until Ribbon Candy is approximately 1½"h. Tie yarn in a knot close to stitched piece. For hanger, tie ends of yarn in a knot 3" above Ribbon Candy and trim ends.

Fig. A

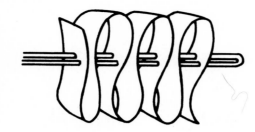

Ribbon Candy
(7 x 78 threads)

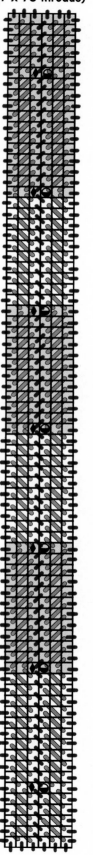

Lollipop Front / Back
(19 x 19 threads) (Work 2)

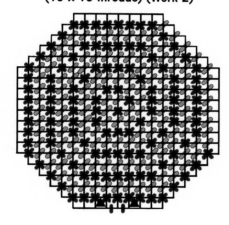

Candy Cane Side A
(11 x 21 threads)

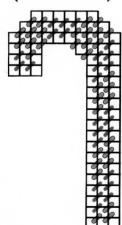

Candy Cane Side B
(11 x 21 threads)

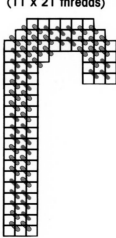

NATIVITY TRIPTYCH

The whole family can share in the wonder of the Holy Birth with this simple Nativity triptych. With its three hinged panels illustrating that wondrous night, the scene will help show children the much-loved story of how the shepherds and wise men came to adore the Baby Jesus so many years ago. They can even take part by moving the freestanding sheep to kneel before the manger.

Skill Level: Intermediate

Size: 12½"w x 11¾"h

Supplies: Worsted weight yarn (refer to color keys), three 10⅝ x 13⅝ sheets of 7 mesh plastic canvas, #16 tapestry needle, Kreinik ⅛"w metallic gold ribbon, and posterboard

Stitches Used: Backstitch, Cross Stitch, French Knot, Gobelin Stitch, Overcast Stitch, and Tent Stitch

Instructions: Follow charts and use required stitches to work Triptych pieces. (**Note:** Backs are not worked). For supports, cut six pieces of posterboard slightly smaller than Center Back. Refer to photo and use tan to join Fronts along long edges. Use lt gold to join Backs along long edges. Use lt gold to join Fronts to Backs along top and side edges. Slide two posterboard supports into each point between Fronts and Backs. Use lt gold to join bottom edges of Fronts to Backs. Refer to photo to glue Star to Center Front. Refer to photo for yarn colors used to join Sheep and Lamb pieces. Refer to photo to tack one Sheep Ear to each Sheep Side. With wrong sides together, match ▲'s to join Sheep Side A to Sheep Side B between ▲'s. Refer to photo to tack Sheep to Sheep Base. Refer to photo to tack one Lamb Ear to each Lamb Side. With wrong sides together, match ●'s to join Lamb Side A to Lamb Side B between ●'s. Refer to photo to tack Lamb to Lamb Base.

▧ white	▧ purple	▨ black
▨ lt gold	▧ lt tan	▥ metallic gold
▧ peach	▧ tan	▧ white 2-ply
▧ pink	▧ beige	▨ orange 2-ply
▨ rust	▧ beige brown	⊙ white 2-ply Fr. Knot
▧ lt blue	▧ dk beige brown	⊙ black 2-ply Fr. Knot
▧ blue	▨ brown	
▧ lt purple	▧ dk brown	

Designed by Dick Martin.

Lamb Side A (10 x 13 threads)

Lamb Side B (13 x 10 threads)

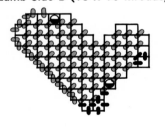

Lamb Base (12 x 12 threads)

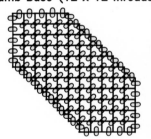

Lamb Ear
(3 x 3 threads)
(Work 2)

Sheep Side A (13 x 16 threads)

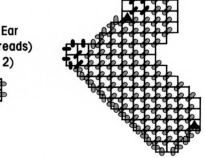

Sheep Side B (16 x 13 threads)

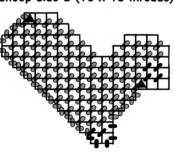

Sheep Base (15 x 15 threads)

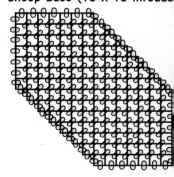

Sheep Ear
(3 x 4 threads)
(Work 2)

Left Front/Back (28 x 65 threads) (Cut 2)

Center Front/Back (28 x 65 threads) (Cut 2)

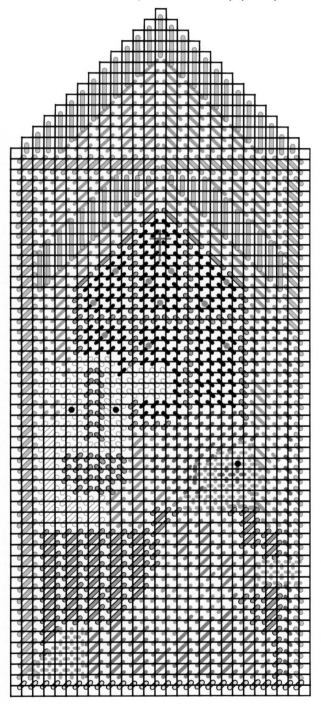
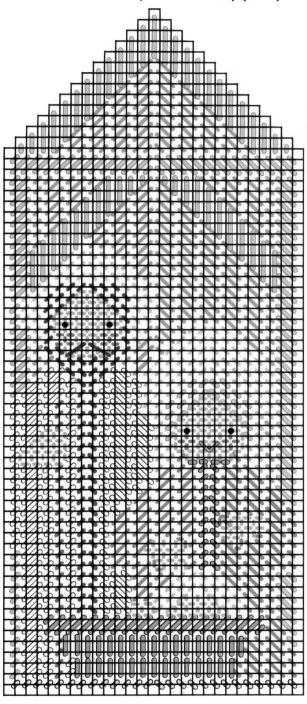

☑ white	☑ orchid	☑ green	☑ dk brown
☑ peach	☑ vy lt purple	☑ dk rust	☑ black
☑ lt gold	☑ dk purple	☑ lt tan	☑ metallic gold
☑ gold	☑ aqua	☑ tan	⊙ aqua 2-ply Fr. Knot
☑ pink	☑ lt green	☑ lt brown	⊙ black 2-ply Fr. Knot

Right Front/Back (28 x 65 threads) (Cut 2)

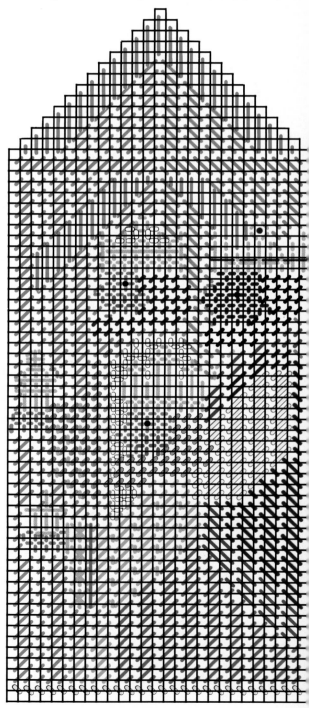

Star (18 x 18 threads)

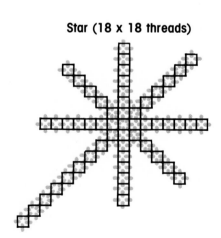

Sweet Little Angel

Clasping a candy cane surprise, this sweet little angel makes a charming package decoration or tree ornament. What a divine idea!

Skill Level: Intermediate

Size: 4"w x 5⅝"h

Supplies: Worsted weight yarn (refer to color key), one 10⅝" x 13⅝" sheet of 7 mesh plastic canvas, and #16 tapestry needle

Stitches Used: Backstitch, French Knot, Gobelin Stitch, Overcast Stitch, Tent Stitch, and Turkey Loop

Instructions: Follow chart and use required stitches to work Angel Candy Cane Holder. Refer to photo to insert candy cane.

Designed by Debbie Tabor.

Angel Candy Cane Holder (36 x 36 threads)

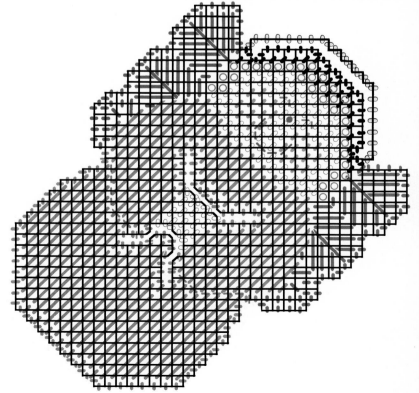

◢ white	◢ pink
◢ lt yellow	◢ dk pink 2-ply
◢ yellow	◢ grey 2-ply
◢ dk yellow	● flesh Fr. Knot
◢ flesh	○ yellow Turkey Loop

Fun and Frosty Snowmen

These frosty friends will bring lots of fun to your holiday table! Dinner guests will love the cute snowman napkin rings, and the two standing snowmen have a special surprise — their heads lift off so you can fill them with candy or other treats for your friends to enjoy.

NAPKIN RING
Skill Level: Advanced
Size: 2¾"w x 4¾"h x1¼"d
Supplies For Four Napkin Rings: Worsted weight yarn (refer to color key), two 10⅝" x 13⅝" sheets of 7 mesh plastic canvas, and #16 tapestry needle
Stitches Used: Backstitch, French Knot, Overcast Stitch, and Tent Stitch

Instructions: Follow charts and use required stitches to work Napkin Ring pieces, leaving stitches in shaded area unworked. Turn Scarf over to work stitches in shaded area. Use color to match stitching area to join Snowman Front to Snowman Back. Refer to photo and use red to tack ends of Scarf together around Snowman. Slide Hat Brim onto Snowman; use black to tack Hat Brim in place. Use white to join bottom edge of Snowman to Ring Top between **x**'s. Use green to join Ring Top and Ring Bottom to Ring Sides along short edges. Use green to join Ring Front and Ring Back to Ring Top, Ring Bottom, and Ring Sides.

SMALL SNOWMAN CONTAINER
Skill Level: Advanced
Size: 4½"w x 6"h x 2¼"d
Supplies: Worsted weight yarn (refer to color key), one 10⅝" x 13⅝" sheet of 7 mesh plastic canvas, and #16 tapestry needle
Stitches Used: Fringe, Gobelin Stitch, Overcast Stitch, and Tent Stitch

Instructions: Follow charts and use required stitches to work Small Snowman Container pieces. Use black and match ▲'s to join Hat Sides to Hat Top. Use black and match **x**'s to join Top Sides to Hat Sides. Use yarn color to match stitching area to join Top Sides, Hat Sides, and Hat Top to Top Front and Top Back. Slide Hat Brim onto Hat; use black to tack Hat Brim in place. Use white and match ♦'s to join Body Sides to Bottom. Use red and match ◓'s to join Scarf Sides to Body Sides. Use yarn color to match stitching area to join Scarf Sides, Body Sides, and Bottom to Body Front and Body Back. Refer to photo and use red to tack Scarf End A and Scarf End B to Scarf Side.

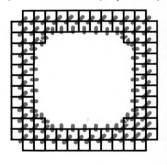

▱	white
▱	red
▱	green
◪	black
⊙	black Fr. Knot
◎	red Fringe

Designed by Dick Martin.

Snowman Front
(12 x 18 threads)

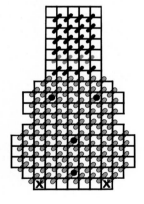

Snowman Back
(12 x 18 threads)

Ring Front/Back
(14 x 14 threads) (Work 2)

Scarf (26 x 26 threads)

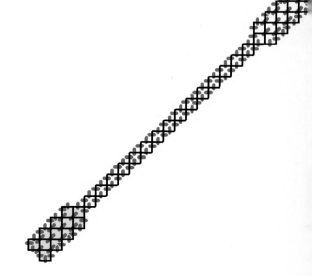

Hat Brim (11 x 6 threads)

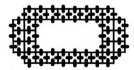

Ring Side
(8 x 12 threads)
(Work 2)

Ring Top/Bottom
(12 x 8 threads)
(Work 2)

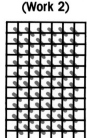

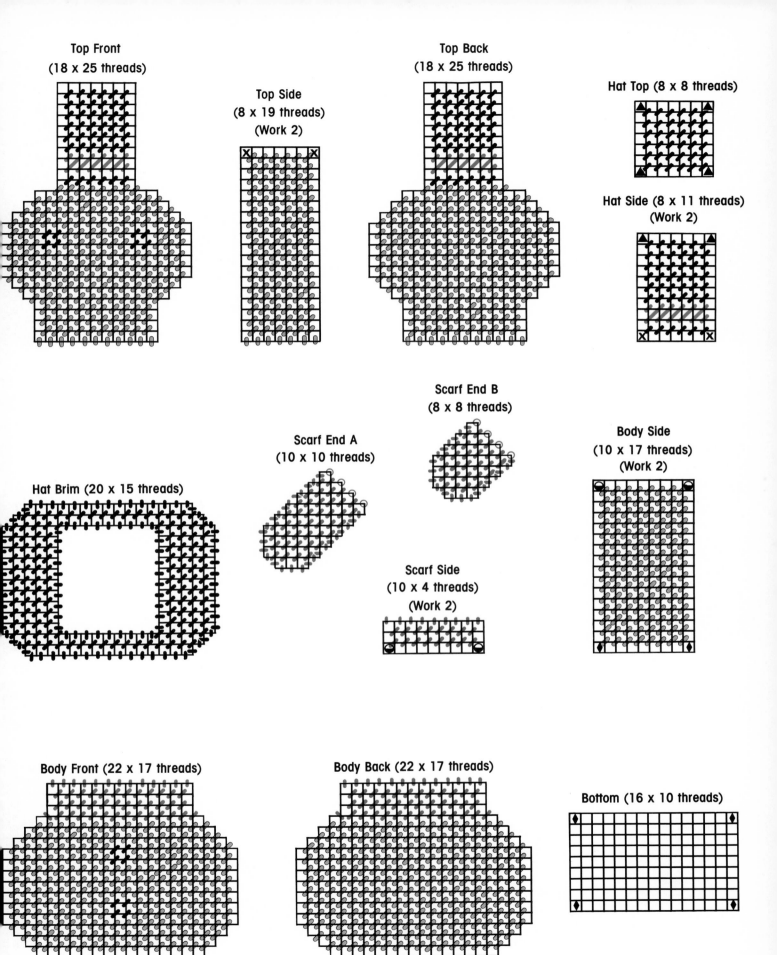

Top Front
(18 x 25 threads)

Top Back
(18 x 25 threads)

Top Side
(8 x 19 threads)
(Work 2)

Hat Top (8 x 8 threads)

Hat Side (8 x 11 threads)
(Work 2)

Scarf End B
(8 x 8 threads)

Scarf End A
(10 x 10 threads)

Hat Brim (20 x 15 threads)

Body Side
(10 x 17 threads)
(Work 2)

Scarf Side
(10 x 4 threads)
(Work 2)

Body Front (22 x 17 threads)

Body Back (22 x 17 threads)

Bottom (16 x 10 threads)

LARGE SNOWMAN CONTAINER

Skill Level: Advanced

Size: 6½"w x 8½"h x 3⅜"d

Supplies: Worsted weight yarn (refer to color key), two 10⅝" x 13⅝" sheets of 7 mesh plastic canvas, and #16 tapestry needle

Stitches Used: Fringe, Gobelin Stitch, Overcast Stitch, and Tent Stitch

Instructions: Follow charts and use required stitches to work Large Snowman Container pieces. Use black and match ▲'s to join Hat Sides to Hat Top. Use black and match **x**'s to join Top Sides to Hat Sides. Use red and match ●'s to join Scarf Sides to Top Sides. Use yarn color to match stitching area to join Scarf Sides, Top Sides, Hat Sides, and Hat Top to Top Front and Top Back. Slide Hat Brim onto Hat; use black to tack Hat Brim in place. Use white and match ♦'s to join Body Sides to Bottom. Use yarn color to match stitching area to join Body Sides and Bottom to Body Front and Body Back. Refer to photo and use red to tack Scarf End A and Scarf End B to Body Side.

Top Front (26 x 33 threads)

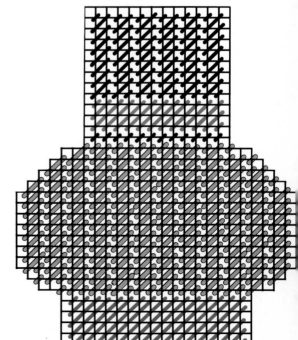

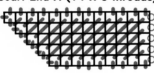 white   green   ⊙ red Fringe

▨ red   ▨ black

Scarf Side (14 x 7 threads) (Work 2)

Scarf End A (14 x 6 threads)

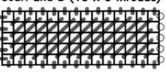

Scarf End B (15 x 6 threads)

Top Back (26 x 33 threads)

Hat Brim (30 x 24 threads)

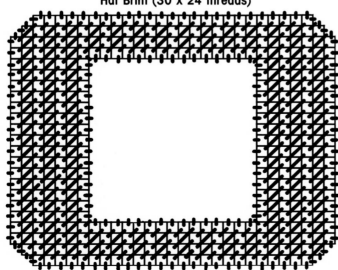

42

Hat Top (14 x 14 threads)

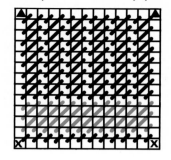

Hat Side (14 x 14 threads) (Work 2)

Top Side (14 x 20 threads) (Work 2)

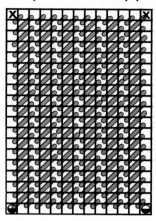

Body Front (34 x 28 threads)

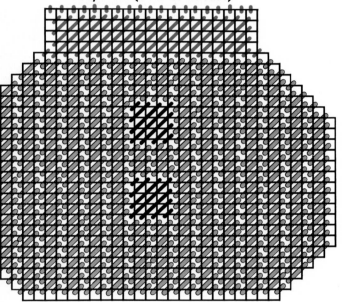

Body Side (16 x 33 threads) (Work 2)

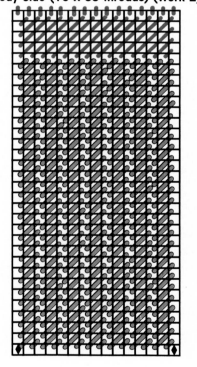

Body Back (34 x 28 threads)

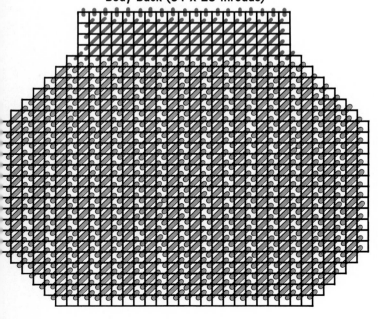

Bottom (24 x 16 threads)

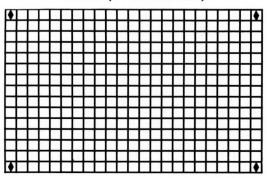

Skiing Santa Cover-up

Our whimsical skiing Santa lends holiday charm to this fun tissue box cover. For added dimension, the jolly gift-giver and some of the trees are stitched separately and attached to the wintry mountain backdrop. Each panel features a different view and a variety of stitches.

Skill Level: Intermediate

Size: 4⅝"w x 5¾"h x 4⅝"d

(Note: Fits a 4¼"w x 5¼"h x 4¼"d boutique tissue box.)

Supplies: Worsted weight yarn (refer to color keys), two 10⅝" x 13⅝" sheets of 7 mesh plastic canvas, #16 tapestry needle, 4" length of 3mm black chenille stem, and clear-drying craft glue

Stitches Used: Alternating Mosaic Stitch, Backstitch, Cashmere Stitch, Cross Stitch, Gobelin Stitch, Overcast Stitch, Tent Stitch, and Turkey Loop

Instructions: Follow charts and use required stitches to work Tissue Box Cover pieces. Use yarn to match stitching area for all joining. Match like symbols to join Sides along long edges. Join Top to Sides. Use white Overcast Stitches to cover unworked edges. For ski pole, refer to photo to bend chenille stem. Refer to photo to glue pieces together.

Designed by Jack Peatman for LuvLee Designs.

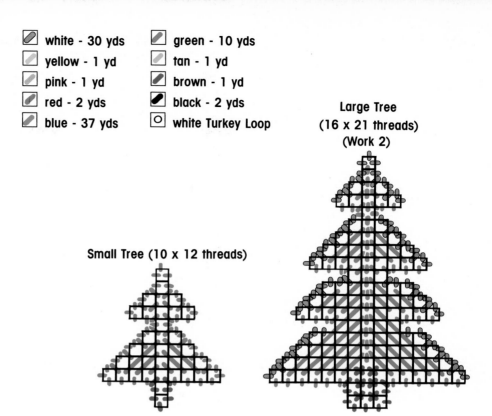

white - 30 yds			green - 10 yds	
yellow - 1 yd			tan - 1 yd	
pink - 1 yd			brown - 1 yd	
red - 2 yds			black - 2 yds	
blue - 37 yds			white Turkey Loop	

Large Tree
(16 x 21 threads)
(Work 2)

Small Tree (10 x 12 threads)

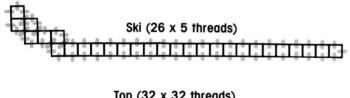

Ski (26 x 5 threads)

Top (32 x 32 threads)

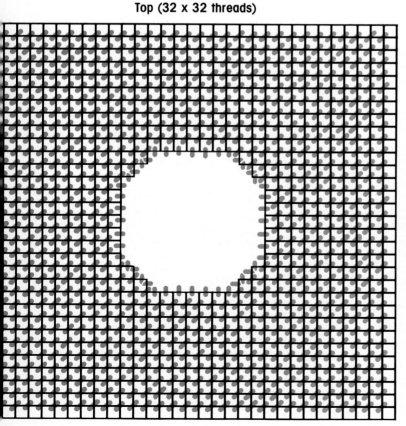

Arm (10 x 7 threads)

Santa (19 x 28 threads)

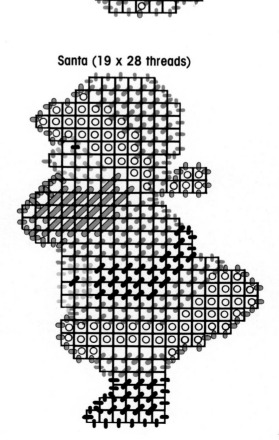

Side B (32 x 37 threads)

Side A (32 x 37 threads)

white
lt purple - 6 yds
purple - 5 yds
blue
blue green - 7 yds
green

46

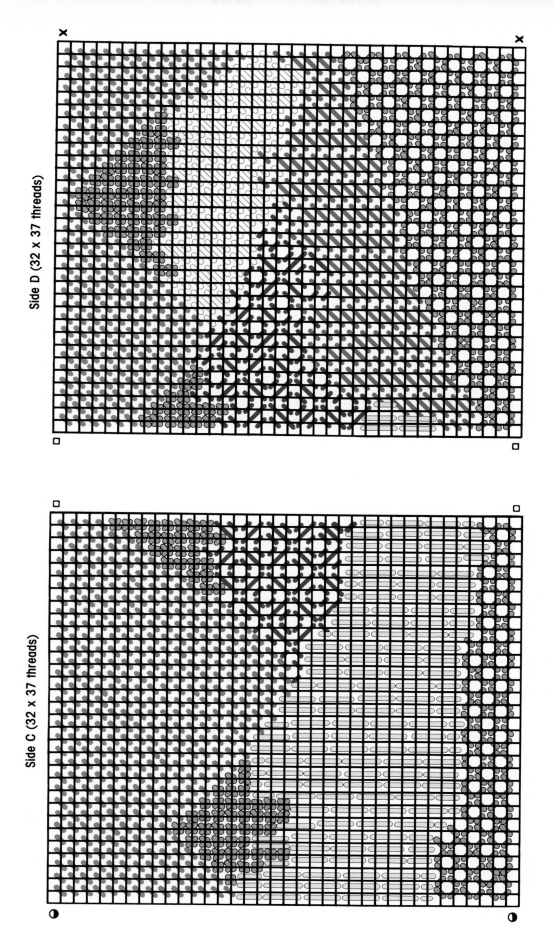

Side D (32 x 37 threads)

Side C (32 x 37 threads)

Olde World Gentlemen

*Add Olde World charm to your Yuletide celebration
with the nostalgic Santa Claus decorations shown
here and on the following pages. Clad in colorful coats
of red, blue, gold, or green, the gentlemen are stitched
with Persian yarn for extra richness. The standing
figures and stacking blocks are created by stitching
the same designs in three different mesh sizes.
The five ornaments, perfect for trimming a tree or
wreath, reflect the same friendly faces that
adorn the old-fashioned blocks.*

SANTA ORNAMENTS

Skill Level: Intermediate
Approx Size: 3⅝"w x 4"h each
Supplies For Set: Paternayan Persian Yarn (refer to color key), one 10⅝" x 13⅝" sheet of 10 mesh plastic canvas, #20 tapestry needle, nylon line, and #26 tapestry needle (for working with nylon line)
Stitches Used: Overcast Stitch and Tent Stitch
Instructions: Follow chart and use required stitches to work Ornament, using desired background color. Use color to match stitching area to work Overcast Stitches to cover unworked edges. For hanger, cut an 8" length of nylon line. Thread nylon line through top of Ornament and tie ends together in a knot 3" above Ornament.

SANTA BLOCKS

Skill Level: Intermediate
7 Mesh Size: 7"w x 7"h x 7"d
10 Mesh Size: 5"w x 5"h x 5"d
14 Mesh Size: 3"w x 3"h x 5"d
Supplies For Set: Paternayan Persian Yarn (refer to color key), two 13⅝" x 22⅝" sheets of 7 mesh plastic canvas, two 10⅝" x 13⅝" sheets of 10 mesh plastic canvas, one 8⅛" x 10⅞" sheet of 14 mesh plastic canvas, and #16, #20, and #24 tapestry needles
Stitches Used: Overcast Stitch and Tent Stitch
Instructions: For each Block, cut six pieces of plastic canvas 49 x 49 threads each. Refer to photo to center and stitch desired Santa Face on each Side. Use desired color Tent Stitches to work backgrounds. (**Note:** We used 900 vy dk red on the 7 mesh Block, 660 vy dk pine green on the 10 mesh Block, and 500 vy dk grey blue on the 14 mesh Block.) Refer to photo to join Sides, forming a Block.

 260 white
 262 ecru
 422 vy dk brown
 453 dk beige
 454 beige
 455 lt beige
 486 vy dk flesh
 490 dk flesh
 494 vy lt flesh
 550 dk blue
 551 blue
 552 lt blue

 660 vy dk pine green
 661 dk pine green
 662 pine green
 663 lt pine green
 731 vy dk gold
 733 dk gold
 735 lt gold
 900 vy dk red
 934 pink
 968 red
 970 lt red
 background color

Santa #1 (35 x 37 threads)

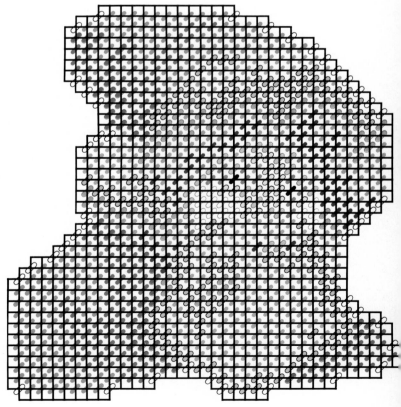

Santa #2 (36 x 37 threads)

Santa #3 (35 x 37 threads)

Santa #4 (35 x 37 threads)

Santa #5 (35 x 37 threads)

STANDING SANTAS

Skill Level: Advanced

7 Mesh Size: 11¼"w x 22"h x 3¾"d
10 Mesh Size: 7½"w x 14¾"h x 2½"d
14 Mesh Size: 5¼"w x 10½"h x 1⅞"d

Supplies For Set: Paternayan Persian Yarn (refer to color keys), three 13⅝" x 22⅝" sheets of 7 mesh plastic canvas, three 10⅝" x 13⅝" sheets of 10 mesh plastic canvas, two 8⅛" x 10⅞" sheets of 14 mesh plastic canvas, #16, #20, and #24 tapestry needles, polyester fiberfill, aquarium gravel, and sealable plastic bags

Stitches Used: Alternating Scotch Stitch, French Knot, Overcast Stitch, and Tent Stitch

Instructions: To create a larger piece of plastic canvas, place two pieces of canvas together with four threads overlapped. Use yarn to tack pieces together until overlapped area is stitched through both thicknesses. (**Note:** Larger canvas will be necessary for 10 mesh size only.) Follow charts and use required stitches to work Front in center of plastic canvas with overlapped area near bottom. Use chart as a guide to cut out Front, leaving one unworked thread around entire stitched area. Use Front as pattern to cut out Back. Turn Back over (head should be on the right). Work Back with 660 vy dk pine green Alternating Scotch Stitches over four threads. With wrong sides together, use vy dk pine green to join Front to Back, leaving bottom edges open. Stuff Standing Santa with polyester fiberfill to within 1" of opening and place bag of aquarium gravel in opening. Fill in remaining space with polyester fiberfill. Use vy dk pine green to join Bottom to Front and Back. **For blue coat,** substitute 550 dk blue for 901 dk red; 551 blue for 968 red; and 552 lt blue for 970 lt red. **For gold coat,** substitute 731 vy dk gold for 901 dk red; 733 dk gold for 968 red; and 735 lt gold for 970 lt red.

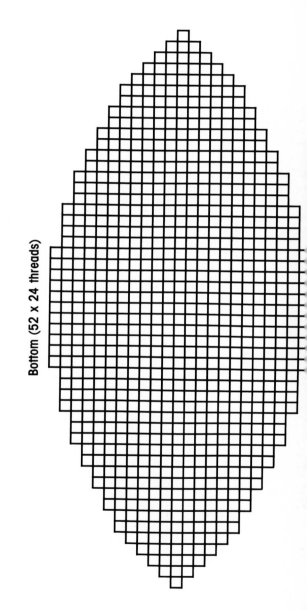

Bottom (52 x 24 threads)

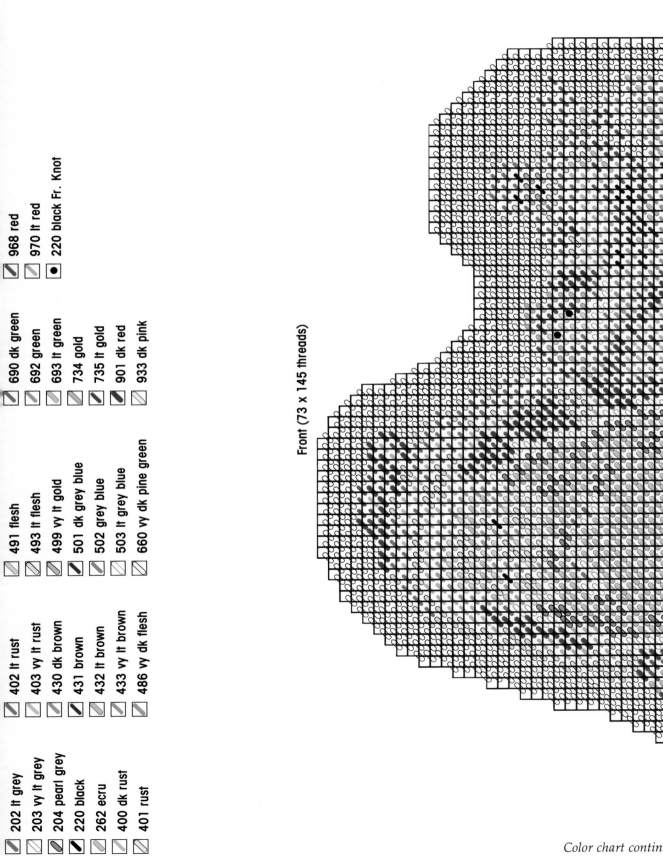

202 lt grey
203 vy lt grey
204 pearl grey
220 black
262 ecru
400 dk rust
401 rust

402 lt rust
403 vy lt rust
430 dk brown
431 brown
432 lt brown
433 vy lt brown
486 vy dk flesh

491 flesh
493 lt flesh
499 vy lt gold
501 dk grey blue
502 grey blue
503 lt grey blue
660 vy dk pine green

690 dk green
692 green
693 lt green
734 gold
735 lt gold
901 dk red
933 dk pink

968 red
970 lt red
220 black Fr. Knot

Front (73 x 145 threads)

Color chart continued on page 56.

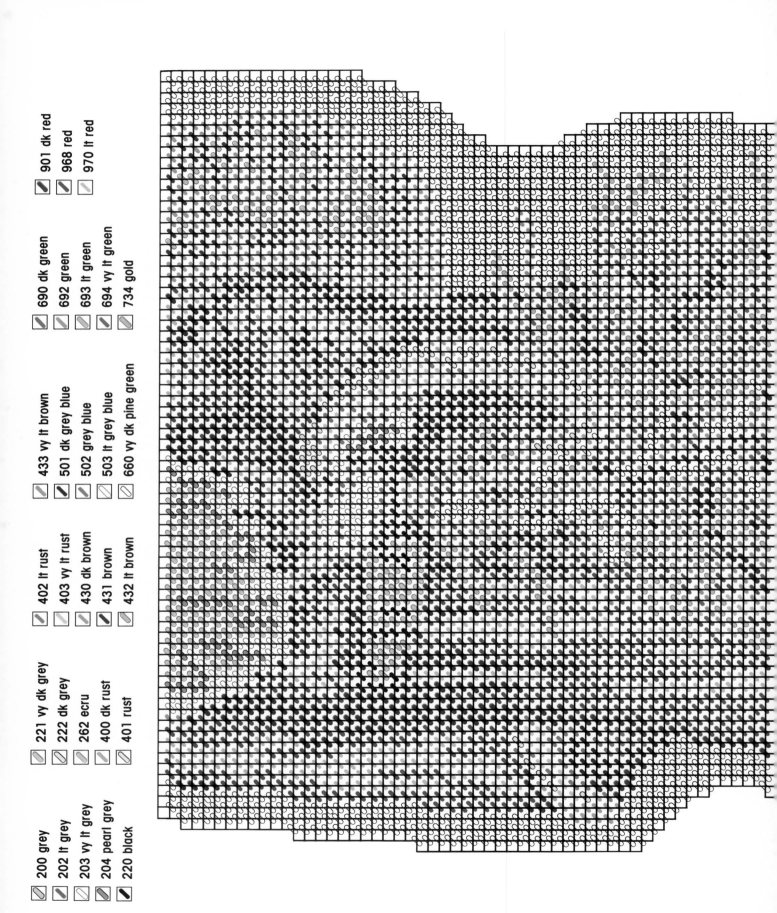

200 grey
202 lt grey
203 vy lt grey
204 pearl grey
220 black

221 vy dk grey
222 dk grey
262 ecru
400 dk rust
401 rust

402 lt rust
403 vy lt rust
430 dk brown
431 brown
432 lt brown

433 vy lt brown
501 dk grey blue
502 grey blue
503 lt grey blue
660 vy dk pine green

690 dk green
692 green
693 lt green
694 vy lt green
734 gold

901 dk red
968 red
970 lt red

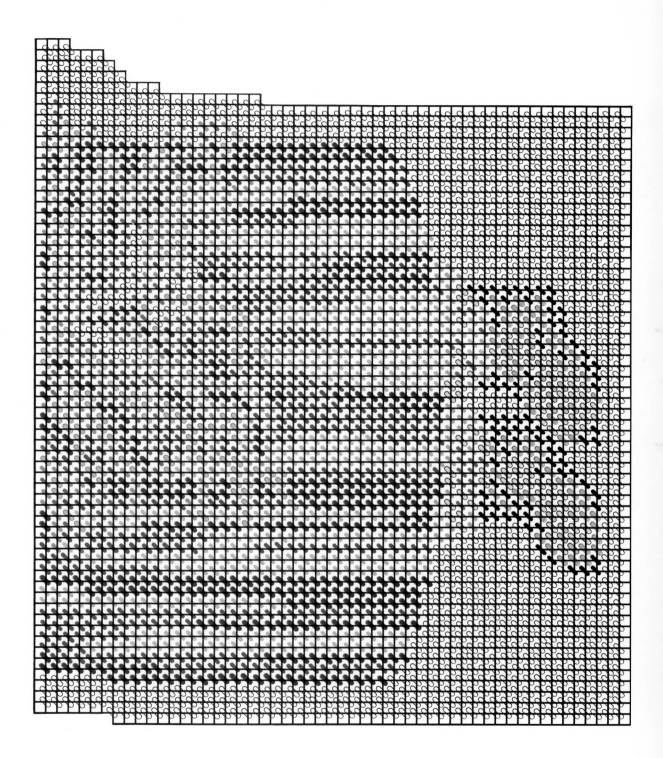

COLORFUL CARDINALS

Add a splash of color to the holidays with a flock of Christmas cardinals! Teamed with natural-looking trims such as bird nests, jute, holly, and pinecones, the bright birds will add a cheery touch to a wreath or tabletop tree.

Skill Level: Beginner
Size: 3¼"w x 1⅞"h x 3"d
Supplies: Worsted weight yarn (refer to color key), one 10⅝" x 13⅝" sheet of 7 mesh plastic canvas, and #16 tapestry needle
Stitches Used: Backstitch, Cross Stitch, French Knot, Gobelin Stitch, Overcast Stitch, and Tent Stitch
Instructions: Follow charts and use required stitches to work Redbird pieces. With wrong sides together, use red to join Wings. With wrong sides together, use yarn color to match stitching area to join Sides. Refer to photo and use red to tack Wings to Sides.

Designed by Jack Peatman for LuvLee Designs.

red
gold
black
● black Fr. Knot

Wings (21 x 10 threads) (Work 2)

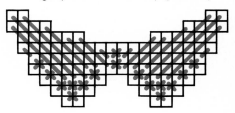

Side A (20 x 12 threads)

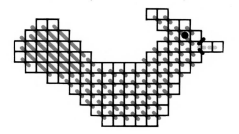

Side B (20 x 12 threads)

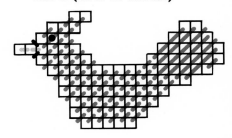

REINDEER FUN

*Striking a variety of poses, Santa's
faithful reindeer are ready to join
in the celebration! Some of them peek
around bright stars, others hug colorful
Christmas balls, and the kiss reindeer
offer candy canes to loved ones! These
whimsical decorations are perfect
for packages or the tree.*

Skill Level: Intermediate

Supplies For One Of Each Ornament:
Worsted weight yarn (refer to color key), Kreinik ⅛"w metallic silver ribbon, one 10⅝" x 13⅝" sheet of 7 mesh plastic canvas, #16 tapestry needle, four 5mm black half round beads, two 9mm brown animal eyes, four 3mm metallic gold beads, two 4mm metallic gold beads, two 6mm black faceted beads, one 8mm black faceted bead, 24" of 1⁄16"w green satin ribbon, nylon line, #26 tapestry needle (for working with nylon line), and clear-drying craft glue

Stitches Used: Backstitch, Overcast Stitch, and Tent Stitch

REINDEER KISS

Size: 3½"w x 4⅛"h x 2½"d

Instructions: Follow charts and use required stitches to work Reindeer Kiss pieces. With right sides facing up, use brown and match ◔'s to join Top to Back along unworked edges of Top. Use brown and match ▲'s to join Bottom to Back along unworked edges. Attach animal eyes to Top at ★'s. For harness, cut a 12" length of satin ribbon. Secure one end of ribbon on wrong side of Back. Refer to photo to thread ribbon through canvas at ■'s and ✳'s. Secure loose end of ribbon on wrong side of Back. Use nylon line to attach 4mm gold beads to Top at ✳'s. Use nylon line to attach 8mm black bead to Top at ◆. For hanger, cut an 8" length of nylon line. Thread nylon line through Kiss and tie ends together in a knot 3" above stitched piece.

REINDEER ORNAMENTS

Approx Size: 4¾"w x 6"h each

Instructions: Follow charts and use required stitches to work Ornament pieces. (**Note:** Refer to photo for alternate colors for Christmas Ball.) Glue half round beads to Reindeer at ★'s. Use nylon line to attach 3mm gold beads to Reindeer at ✳'s. Use nylon line to attach 6mm black bead to Reindeer at ◆. Refer to photo to glue Reindeer to Star or Christmas Ball. Match □'s to glue Hooves to Star or Christmas Ball. For hanger, cut an 8" length of nylon line. Thread nylon line through Reindeer and tie ends together in a knot 3" above stitched piece.

Designed by Darla Fanton.

Back (23 x 23 threads)

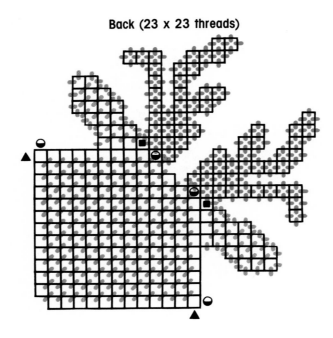

Top (14 x 14 threads)

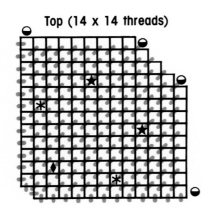

Bottom (14 x 14 threads)

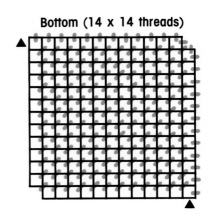

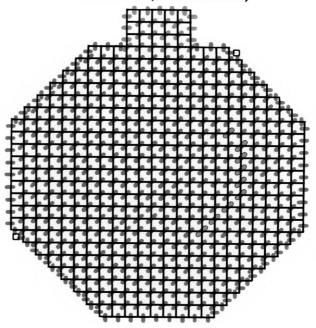	white
	yellow
	pink
	red
	lt brown
	brown
	black
	metallic silver ribbon
	green ribbon

Christmas Ball (24 x 26 threads)

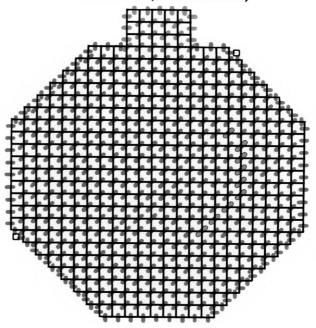

Reindeer (22 x 22 threads)

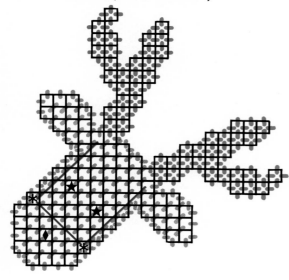

Hoof (5 x 5 threads) (Work 2)

Star (29 x 29 threads)

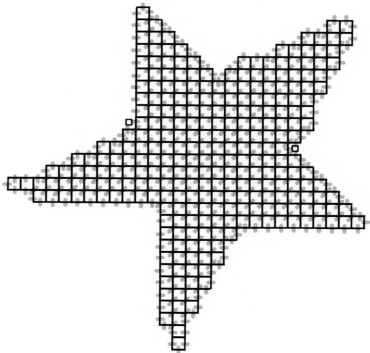

63

MANGER IN MINIATURE

Worked in miniature, this tiny Nativity ornament serves as a gentle reminder of the true meaning of Christmas.

Skill Level: Intermediate
Size: 3½"w x 2⅝"h x 2"d
Supplies: Worsted weight yarn (refer to color key), Kreinik ⅛"w metallic gold ribbon, one 10⅝" x 13⅝" sheet of 7 mesh plastic canvas, #16 tapestry needle, 8" of nylon line, #26 tapestry needle (for working with nylon line), and clear-drying craft glue
Stitches Used: Backstitch, Cross Stitch, Gobelin Stitch, Overcast Stitch, and Tent Stitch

Instructions: Follow charts and use required stitches to work Ornament pieces. Use brown to join Sides to Back. Use tan to join Bottom to Back and Sides. Use brown Overcast Stitches to cover unworked edges of Sides. Use tan to join Roof pieces between ◒'s. Use tan to join Roof to Back. Use tan Overcast Stitches to cover unworked edges of Roof. Use tan to tack Roof to Sides. Refer to photo to glue Star to Roof. Slide notches of Manger pieces together. Use brown to tack Manger pieces together. Refer to photo to glue Jesus to Manger. Use blue to join Mary along unworked edges. Use green to join Joseph along unworked edges. Refer to photo to glue Joseph, Mary, and Manger to Bottom. For hanger, thread nylon line through Roof at ▲'s. Tie ends of nylon line together in a knot 3" above Roof.

Designed by Kathy Bidler.

Color key:
- white
- flesh
- lt blue
- blue
- lt green
- green
- tan
- brown
- metallic gold ribbon

Joseph (10 x 10 threads)

Mary (9 x 9 threads)

Jesus (3 x 6 threads)

Manger (6 x 6 threads) (Work 2)

Star (6 x 7 threads)

Roof (12 x 16 threads) (Work 2)

Back (16 x 17 threads)

Side (11 x 10 threads) (Work 2)
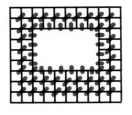

Bottom (16 x 11 threads)
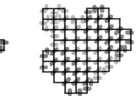

Carousel Horses
of Yesteryear

Prancing around on a Christmas tree or wreath, these old-fashioned carousel horses are wonderful reminders of bygone days. The dainty ornaments are stitched with fancy metallic braid in soft pastel colors to add extra sparkle to your Yuletide celebration.

Skill Level: Advanced

Size: 4"w x 4¼"h

Supplies: Kreinik #16 medium braid (refer to color keys), one 8⅛" x 10⅞" sheet of 14 mesh plastic canvas, and #22 tapestry needle

Stitches Used: Backstitch, Gobelin Stitch, Overcast Stitch, and Tent Stitch

Instructions: Follow charts and use required stitches to work Sides. With wrong sides together, use braid color to match stitching area to join Side A to Side B along unworked edges.

Designed by Carole Rodgers.

Side A (45 x 60 threads)

66

WHITE HORSE

▨	002 gold
▨	005 black
▨	006 blue
▨	024 fuchsia
▨	026 amethyst
▨	032 pearl

PINK HORSE

▨	002 gold
▨	005 black
▨	006 blue
▨	007 pink
▨	024 fuchsia
▨	026 amethyst

BLUE HORSE

▨	002 gold
▨	005 black
▨	006 blue
▨	014 sky blue
▨	024 fuchsia
▨	026 amethyst

Side B (45 x 60 threads)

Merry Santa Tree Topper

Waving merrily from atop the tree, this cute fellow will add to the fun of the season. He's lightly stuffed, so he looks as ''well-rounded'' as the real Santa!

Skill Level: Intermediate

Size: 10¼"w x 16½"h x 1¼"d

Supplies: Worsted weight yarn (refer to color key), three 10⅝" x 13⅝" sheets of 7 mesh plastic canvas, #16 tapestry needle, 15½" length of ¼" dia wooden dowel, and tissue paper

Stitches Used: Backstitch, Cross Stitch, French Knot, Gobelin Stitch, Overcast Stitch, and Tent Stitch

Instructions: Follow charts and use required stitches to work Santa Tree Topper pieces. (**Note:** Back is not worked.) Refer to **Fig. A** to place dowel on Back. Use white to stitch dowel to Back. Refer to photo for yarn color used to join Face to Front between **x**'s. Place Front and Back together with dowel between pieces. Use white and work through three thicknesses to join sides of Face to Front and Back between ▲'s. Match ■'s to place Arm A on Front and Back. Match ●'s to place Arm B on Front and Back. Use yarn color to match stitching area to join Front to Back, joining Arms in place and leaving areas between ★'s open. Use tissue paper to lightly stuff Santa. Use color to match stitching area to join Front to Back between ★'s. Refer to photo and use white to tack Candy Cane to Arm B and Front.

Designed by Dick Martin.

Fig. A

Candy Cane (14 x 30 threads)

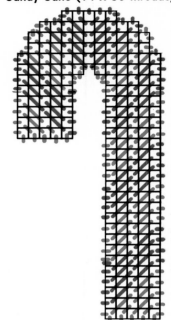

	white		green
	peach		black
	pink	●	green Fr. Knot
	red		

Face (28 x 19 threads)

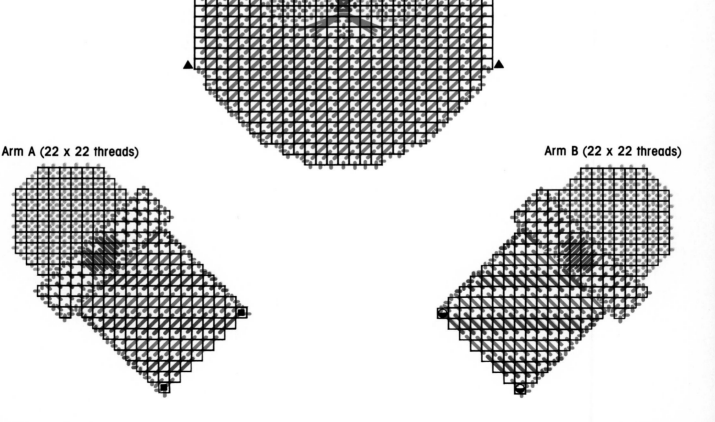

Arm A (22 x 22 threads)

Arm B (22 x 22 threads)

70

Front/Back (58 x 79 threads)
(Cut 2, Work 1)

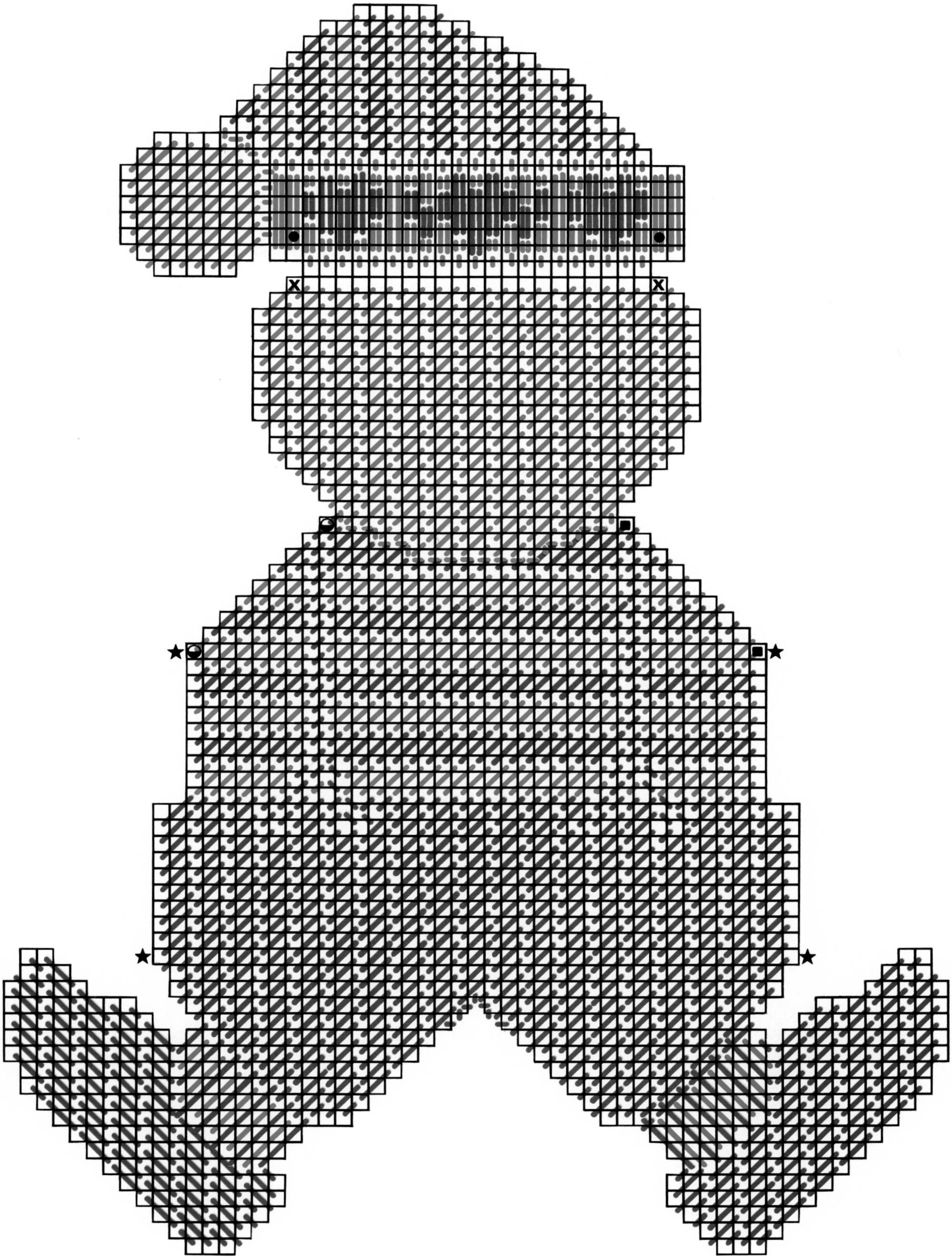

Elegant Snowflakes

Capture the wintry elegance of snowflakes with the icy accents shown here and on the following pages. An intricate three-dimensional snowflake tops the tree with frosty beauty; coordinating ornaments continue the theme. Pure white snowflakes glisten against a background of deep blue on a boutique tissue box cover and a miniature basket.

SNOWFLAKE TREE TOPPER

Skill Level: Advanced
Size: 9¼"w x 9¼"h x ¾"d
Supplies: White worsted weight yarn, two 10⅝" x 13⅝" sheets of 7 mesh plastic canvas, #16 tapestry needle, nylon line, #26 tapestry needle (for working with nylon line), 12½" length of ³⁄₁₆" dia wooden dowel, 6mm pearl beads, and clear-drying craft glue
Stitches Used: Backstitch, Overcast Stitch, and Tent Stitch
Instructions: Follow charts and use required stitches to work Snowflake Tree Topper pieces. Refer to **Fig. A** to alternately join Top A and Top B pieces, forming a ring. Use nylon line to sew beads to Tree Topper pieces. Cut an 80" length of white yarn. Glue the end of yarn to one end of dowel. Wrap the yarn around the dowel to cover 7½" of dowel. Cut off excess yarn and glue remaining yarn end to dowel. Refer to photo to glue Bottom to yarn on dowel. Refer to photo to glue Middle to Bottom. Refer to photo to glue Top to Middle.

Fig. A

TISSUE BOX COVER

Skill Level: Beginner
Size: 4¾"w x 5¾"h x 4¾"d
(**Note:** Fits a 4¼"w x 5¼"h x 4¼"d boutique tissue box.)
Supplies: Worsted weight yarn (refer to color key), two 10⅝" x 13⅝" sheets of 7 mesh plastic canvas, #16 tapestry needle, 4mm pearl beads, and clear-drying craft glue
Stitches Used: Backstitch, Overcast Stitch, and Tent Stitch
Instructions: Follow charts and use required stitches to work Tissue Box Cover pieces. Use blue to join pieces. Join Sides along long edges. Join Top to Sides. Glue beads to Tissue Box Cover.

◹	white
★	6mm pearl bead

Middle (48 x 48 threads)

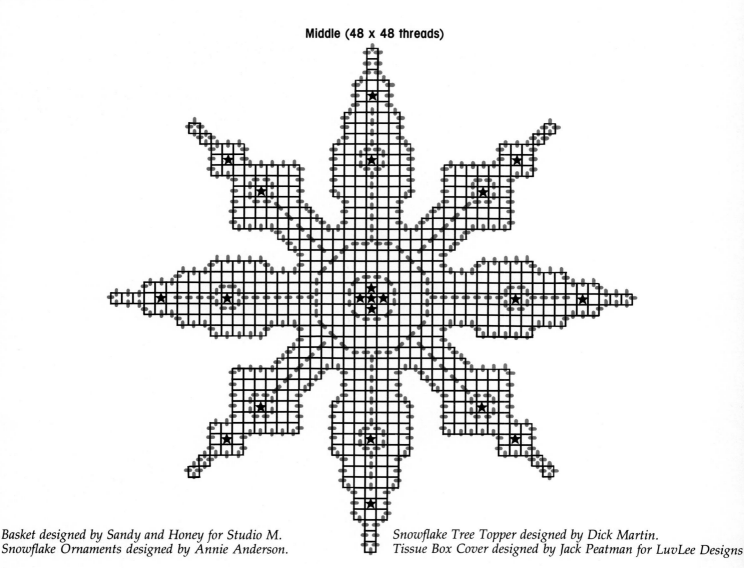

Basket designed by Sandy and Honey for Studio M.
Snowflake Ornaments designed by Annie Anderson.

Snowflake Tree Topper designed by Dick Martin.
Tissue Box Cover designed by Jack Peatman for LuvLee Designs

76

Top A
(7 x 7 threads) (Work 8)

Top B
(6 x 6 threads) (Work 8)

Bottom (62 x 62 threads)

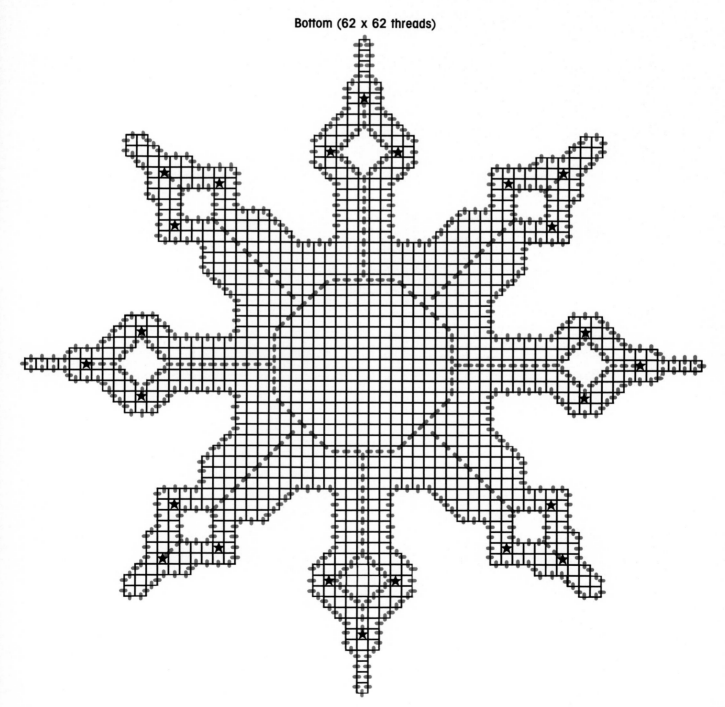

SNOWFLAKE ORNAMENTS

Skill Level: Beginner

Size: 3⅝"w x 3⅝"h each

Supplies: White worsted weight yarn, one 10⅝" x 13⅝" sheet of 7 mesh plastic canvas, #16 tapestry needle, nylon line, #24 tapestry needle (for working with nylon line), and 4mm pearl beads

Stitches Used: Backstitch, Cross Stitch, Gobelin Stitch, and Tent Stitch

Instructions: Follow chart and use required stitches to work Snowflake Ornament. Use nylon line to sew beads to Ornament. For hanger, thread 8" of nylon line through top of Ornament and tie ends together 3" above Ornament.

BASKET

Skill Level: Intermediate

Size: 2½"w x 3"h x 2"d

Supplies: Worsted weight yarn (refer to color key), one 10⅝" x 13⅝" sheet of 7 mesh plastic canvas, 4mm pearl beads, 24" of ¼"w white satin ribbon, and clear-drying craft glue

Stitches Used: Backstitch, Gobelin Stitch, Overcast Stitch, and Tent Stitch

Instructions: Follow charts and use required stitches to work Basket pieces. Refer to photo and use blue to join Sides to Front & Back. Refer to photo and use blue to join Bottom to Sides and Front & Back. Refer to photo to glue Snowflake to Front. Glue pearl beads to Snowflake. Cut ribbon into three 8" lengths. Tie each length of ribbon into a bow and trim ends. Refer to photo to glue bows to Basket.

| ✔ white | ⁄ blue | ★ 4mm pearl bead |

Tissue Box Cover Top (32 x 32 threads)

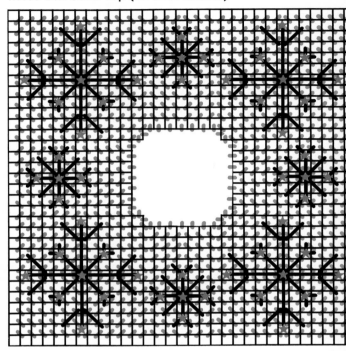

Basket Side
(11 x 11 threads) (Work 2)

Snowflake
(16 x 16 threads)

Basket Front & Back
(16 x 44 threads)

Basket Bottom (16 x 11 threads)

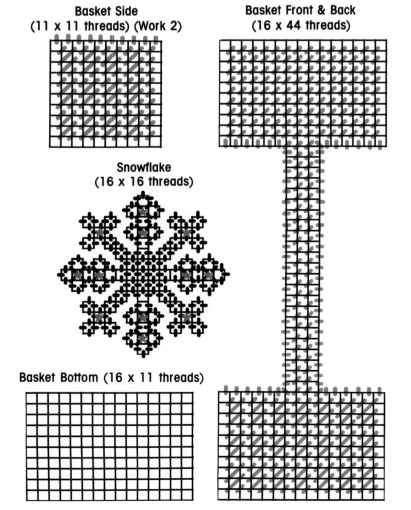

Tissue Box Cover Side (32 x 38 threads) (Work 4)

Snowflake Ornaments
(25 x 25 threads each)

ST. NICK STOCKING

This elegant Christmas stocking is destined to become a treasured heirloom. Persian yarn lends extra richness to the nostalgic design, which was adapted from an antique postcard. Charming finishing touches include red velvet cording along the top, a satin ribbon hanger, and a shiny jingle bell for St. Nick's cap.

Skill Level: Intermediate

Size: 9⅜"w x 16½"h

Supplies: Paternayan Persian Yarn or worsted weight yarn (refer to color key), two 12" x 18" sheets of 7 mesh plastic canvas, #16 tapestry needle, 16" square of red velveteen fabric, 16" of ¼" dia cord, ⅝" dia jingle bell, 6" of ⅝"w red satin ribbon, sewing needle, and thread

Stitches Used: Alternating Scotch Stitch, Backstitch, Overcast Stitch, and Tent Stitch

Instructions: Follow charts and use required stitches to work Stocking Front in center of one sheet of plastic canvas. Use 1-ply Paternayan Persian Yarn or 2-ply worsted weight yarn for Backstitch. Use chart as a guide to cut out Stocking Front, leaving one unworked thread around entire stitched area. Use Stocking Front as pattern to cut out Stocking Back. Turn Stocking Back over (toe should be on the left). Work Stocking Back with 512 blue Alternating Scotch Stitches over four threads. Work Overcast Stitch in 512 blue to cover top edges of Stocking Front and Stocking Back. Refer to photo to sew jingle bell to Stocking Front. With wrong sides together, refer to photo and use yarn color to match stitching area to join Stocking Front to Stocking Back along unworked edges. Refer to Cording Instructions to make fabric covered cording. Refer to photo to tack ribbon to wrong side of Stocking Back. Refer to photo to sew cording to top edges of Stocking Front and Back.

Cording Instructions: Cut a 16" x 2" bias strip from fabric. Place cord on center of wrong side of fabric strip. Fold one long edge of fabric strip over cord and align long edges of fabric strip. Stitch fabric close to cord.

900 dk red - 5 yds
945 pink - 2 yds
968 red - 6 yds
970 lt red - 6 yds

455 lt beige - 12 yds
485 dk flesh - 2 yds
486 flesh - 2 yds
492 lt flesh 2 yds
511 dk blue - 1 yd
512 blue - 120 yds

220 black - 1 yd
260 white - 18 yds
262 ecru - 18 yds
430 brown - 1 yd
453 dk beige - 5 yds
454 beige - 8 yds

Stocking Front/Back (62 x 96 threads)

82

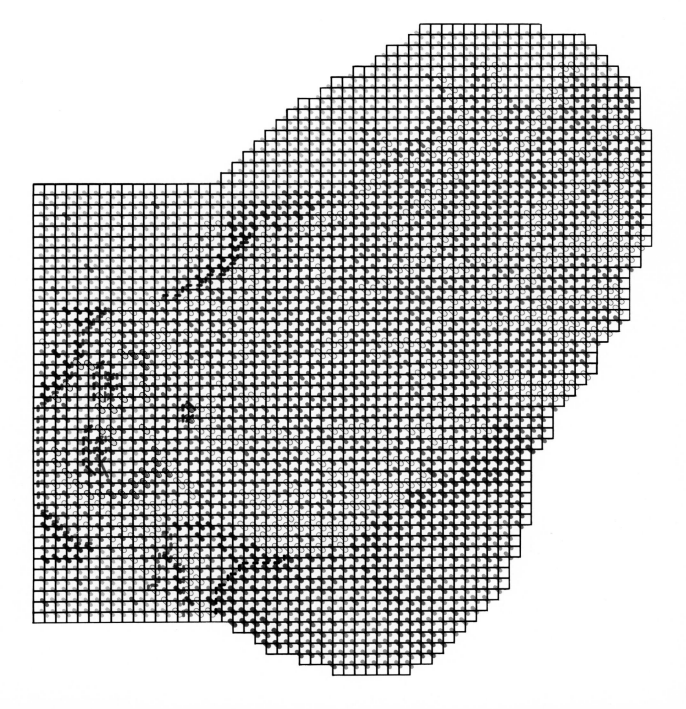

An Old-fashioned Noel

Reminiscent of old-fashioned alphabet blocks, these lovely candle holders foretell a sweet Noel. Each one features an ornate letter stitched in Christmas red or green, a metallic braid border, and a shimmering gold bow.

Skill Level: Beginner

Size: 4½"w x 5"h x 2¾"d each

Supplies: Worsted weight yarn (refer to color key), four 10⅝" x 13⅝" sheets of 7 mesh plastic canvas, Kreinik Gold Cable 002P, #16 tapestry needle, four 1" dia brass candle cups, four 1 yard lengths of 2"w gold mesh ribbon, silk evergreen sprigs, and clear-drying craft glue or hot glue gun and glue sticks

Stitches Used: Backstitch, Cross Stitch, Gobelin Stitch, Overcast Stitch, and Tent Stitch

Instructions: Follow charts and use required stitches to work Holder pieces. Refer to photo to work four additional Sides and two additional Tops, reversing red and green. Refer to photo for yarn colors used to join pieces. (**Note:** Centers of Tops and Sides should match letters on Front.) Join Front and Back to Sides. Match ▲'s to join Top to Front, Back, and Sides. Join Bottom to Front, Back, and Sides. Glue candle cup in opening of Top. Tie each length of ribbon in a bow and trim ends. Refer to photo to glue bow and evergreen sprigs to Tops.

Designed By Jack Peatman for LuvLee Designs.

Top (30 x 18 threads) (Cut 4, Work 2)

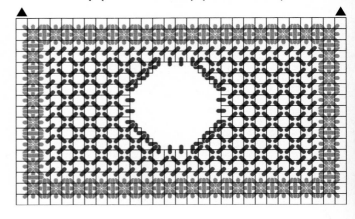

Back (30 x 32 threads) (Work 4)

Side (18 x 32 threads) (Cut 8, Work 4)

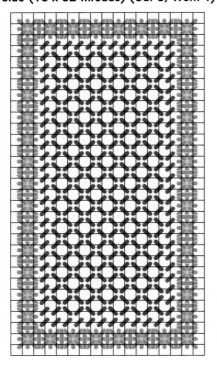

Bottom (30 x 18 threads) (Cut 4)

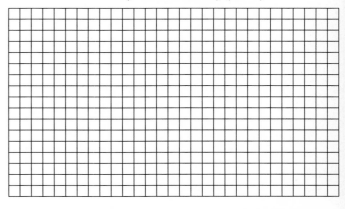

N Front (30 x 32 threads)

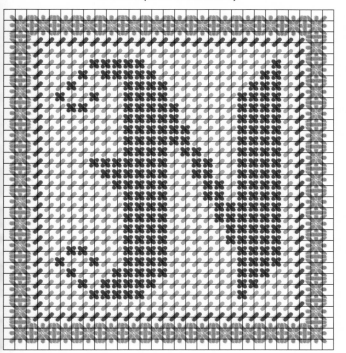

O Front (30 x 32 threads)

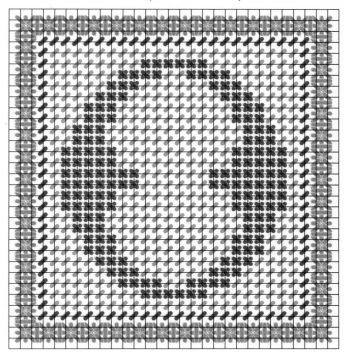

E Front (30 x 32 threads)

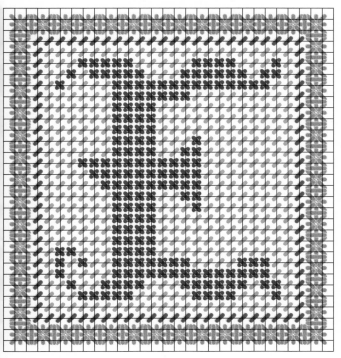

L Front (30 x 32 threads)

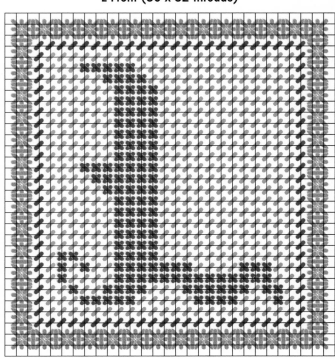

HANDSOME YULETIDE MUG

Diamonds accented with gleaming gold ribbon add elegance to this handsome Yuletide mug. The traditional bargello needlepoint pattern is so easy to stitch that you'll want to make this pretty mug again and again — for holiday gifts and for yourself.

Skill Level: Beginner
Size: 3¼"h x 3"dia
Supplies: Worsted weight yarn (refer to color key), Kreinik ⅛"w metallic gold ribbon, one 10⅝" x 13⅝" sheet of 10 mesh plastic canvas, #20 tapestry needle, and Crafter's Pride® Stitch-A-Mug
Stitches Used: Gobelin Stitch and Overcast Stitch
Instructions: Follow thread count to cut plastic canvas piece. Follow chart and use required stitches to work Mug Insert. Refer to photo and repeat charted pattern until Mug Insert is completed. Use green Overcast Stitches to cover long unworked edges. Use green to join short edges, forming a cylinder. Place Mug Insert into Stitch-A-Mug, aligning joined edges with mug handle. Remove stitched piece before washing mug.

- red
- green
- metallic gold ribbon

Mug Insert (95 x 36 threads)

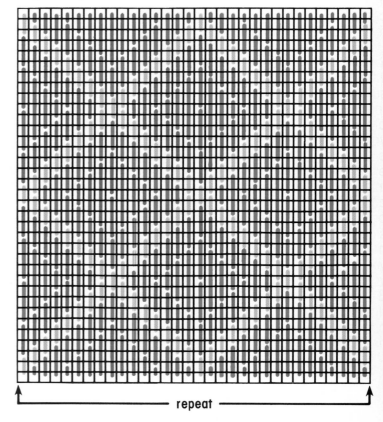

← repeat →

GENERAL INSTRUCTIONS

SELECTING PLASTIC CANVAS

Plastic canvas is a molded, nonwoven canvas made from clear or colored plastic. The canvas consists of "threads" and "holes." The threads aren't actually "threads" since the canvas is nonwoven, but it seems to be an accurate description of the straight lines of the canvas. The holes, as you would expect, are the spaces between the threads. The threads are often referred to in the project instructions, especially when cutting out plastic canvas pieces. The instructions for stitches will always refer to holes when explaining where to place your needle to make a stitch.

TYPES OF CANVAS

The main difference between types of plastic canvas is the mesh size. Mesh size refers to the number of holes in one inch of canvas. The most common mesh sizes are 5 mesh, 7 mesh, 10 mesh, and 14 mesh. Five mesh means that there are 5 holes in every inch of canvas. Likewise, there are 7 holes in every inch of 7 mesh canvas, 10 holes in every inch of 10 mesh canvas, and 14 holes in every inch of 14 mesh canvas. Seven mesh canvas is the most popular size for the majority of projects.

Your project supply list will tell you what size mesh you need to buy. Be sure to use the mesh size the project instructions recommend. If your project calls for 7 mesh canvas and you use 10 mesh, your finished project will be much smaller than expected. For example, say your instructions tell you to use 7 mesh canvas to make a boutique tissue box cover. You will need to cut each side 30 x 38 threads so they will measure 4½" x 5¾" each. But if you were using 10 mesh canvas your sides would only measure 3" x 3⅞"! Needless to say, your tissue box cover from 10 mesh canvas would not fit a boutique tissue box.

Most plastic canvas is made from clear plastic, but colored canvas is also available. Colored plastic is ideal when you don't want to stitch the entire background.

When buying canvas, you may find that some canvas is firm and rigid while other canvas is softer and more pliable. To decide which type of canvas is right for your project, think of how the project will be used. If you are making a box or container, you will want to use firmer canvas so that the box will be sturdy and not buckle after handling. If you are making a tissue box cover, you will not need the firmer canvas because the tissue box will support the canvas and prevent warping. Softer canvas is better for projects that require a piece of canvas to be bent before it is joined to another piece.

AMOUNT OF CANVAS

The project supply list usually tells you how much canvas you will need to complete the project. When buying your canvas, remember that several different manufacturers produce plastic canvas. Therefore, there are often slight variations in canvas, such as different thicknesses of threads or a small difference in mesh size. Because of these variations, try to buy enough canvas for your entire project at the same time and place. As a general rule, it is always better to buy too much canvas and have leftovers than to run out of canvas before you finish your project. By buying a little extra canvas, you not only allow for mistakes, but have extra canvas for practicing your stitches. Scraps of canvas are also excellent for making magnets and other small projects.

SELECTING YARN

You're probably thinking, "How do I select my yarn from the thousands of choices available?" Well, we have a few hints to help you choose the perfect yarns for your project and your budget.

TYPES OF YARN

The first question to ask when choosing yarn is, "How will my project be used?" If your finished project will be handled or used a lot, such as a coaster or magnet, you will want to use a durable, washable yarn. We highly recommend acrylic or nylon yarn for plastic canvas. It can be washed repeatedly and holds up well to frequent usage and handling. If your finished project won't be handled or used frequently, such as a framed picture or a bookend, you are not limited to washable yarns.

Cost may also be a factor in your yarn selection. There again, acrylic yarn is a favorite because it is reasonably priced and comes in a wide variety of colors. However, if your project is something extra special, you may want to spend a little more on wool yarn to get certain shades of color.

The types of yarns available are endless and each grouping of yarn has its own characteristics and uses. The following is a brief description of some common yarns used for plastic canvas.

Worsted Weight Yarn - This yarn may be found in acrylic, wool, wool blends, and a variety of other fiber contents. Worsted weight yarn is the most popular yarn used for 7 mesh plastic canvas because one strand covers the canvas very well. This yarn is inexpensive and comes in a wide range of colors. Worsted weight yarn has four plies which are twisted together to form one strand. When the instructions call for "2-ply" or "1-ply" yarn, you will need to separate a strand of yarn into its four plies and use only the number of plies indicated in the instructions.

Sport Weight Yarn - This yarn has three thin plies which are twisted together to form one strand. Like worsted weight yarn, sport weight yarn comes in a variety of fiber contents. The color selection in sport weight yarn is more limited than in other types of yarns. You may want to use a double strand of sport weight yarn for better coverage of your 7 mesh canvas. When you plan on doubling your yarn, remember to double the yardage called for in the instructions too. Since sport weight yarn must be doubled to completely cover 7 mesh canvas, you may prefer to use other types of yarns.

Tapestry Yarn - This is a thin wool yarn. Because tapestry yarn is available in a wider variety of colors than other yarns, it may be used when several shades of the same color are desired. For example, if you need five shades of pink to stitch a flower, you may choose tapestry yarn for a better blending of colors. Tapestry yarn is ideal for working on 10 mesh canvas. However, it is a more expensive yarn and requires two strands to cover 7 mesh canvas. Projects made with tapestry yarn cannot be washed.

Persian Wool - This is a wool yarn which is made up of three loosely twisted plies. The plies should be separated and realigned before you thread your needle. Like tapestry yarn, Persian yarn has more shades of each color from which to choose. It also has a nap similar to the nap of velvet. To determine the direction of the nap, run the yarn through your fingers. When you rub "with the nap," the yarn is smooth; but when you rub "against the nap," the yarn is rough. For smoother and prettier stitches on your project, stitching should be done "with the nap." The yarn fibers will stand out when stitching is done "against the nap." Because of the wool content, you cannot wash projects made with Persian yarn.

Pearl Cotton - Sometimes #3 pearl cotton is used on plastic canvas to give it a dressy, lacy look. It is not meant to cover 7 mesh canvas completely but to enhance it. Pearl cotton works well on 10 mesh canvas when you want your needlework to have a satiny sheen. If you cannot locate #3 pearl cotton in your area, you can substitute twelve strands of embroidery floss.

Embroidery Floss - Occasionally embroidery floss is used to add small details such as eyes or mouths on 7 mesh canvas. Twelve strands of embroidery floss are recommended for covering 10 mesh canvas. Use six strands to cover 14 mesh canvas.

COLORS

Choosing colors can be fun, but sometimes a little difficult. Your project will tell you what yarn colors you will need. When you begin searching for the recommended colors, you may be slightly overwhelmed by the different shades of each color. Here are a few guidelines to consider when choosing your colors.

Consider where you are going to place the finished project. If the project is going in a particular room in your house, match your yarn to the room's colors.

Try not to mix very bright colors with dull colors. For example, if you're stitching a project using country colors, don't use a bright Christmas red with country blues and greens. Instead, use a maroon or country red. Likewise, if you are stitching a bright tissue box cover for a child's room, don't use country blue with bright red, yellow, and green.

Some projects require several shades of a color, such as shades of red for a Santa. Be sure your shades blend well together.

Sometimes, you may have trouble finding three or four shades of a color. If you think your project warrants the extra expense, you can usually find several shades of a color available in tapestry or Persian yarn.

Remember, you don't have to use the colors suggested in the color key. If you find a blue tissue box cover that you really like, but your house is decorated in pink, change the colors in the tissue box cover to pink!

AMOUNTS

Some projects will list yardages in the project instructions; however many do not. A handy way of estimating yardages is to make a yarn yardage estimator. Cut a 1 yard piece of yarn for each different stitch used in your project. For each stitch, work as many stitches as you can with the 1 yard length of yarn.

To use your yarn yardage estimator, count the number of stitches you were able to make, say 72 Tent Stitches. Now look at the chart for the project you want to make. Estimate the number of ecru Tent Stitches on the chart, say 150. Now divide the estimated number of ecru stitches by the actual number stitched with a yard of yarn. One hundred fifty divided by 72 is approximately two. So you will need about two yards of ecru yarn to make your project. Repeat this for all stitches and yarn colors. To allow for repairs and practice stitches, purchase extra yardage of each color. If you have yarn left over, remember that scraps of yarn are perfect for small projects such as magnets or when you need just a few inches of a particular color for another project.

In addition to purchasing an adequate amount of each color of yarn, it is also important to buy all of the yarn you need to complete your project at the same time. Yarn often varies in the amount of dye used to color the yarn. Although the variation may be slight when yarns from two different dye lots are held together, the variation is usually very apparent in a stitched piece.

SELECTING NEEDLES
TYPES OF NEEDLES
Stitching on plastic canvas should be done with a blunt needle called a tapestry needle. Tapestry needles are sized by numbers; the higher the number, the smaller the needle. The correct size needle to use depends on the canvas mesh size and the yarn thickness. The needle should be small enough to allow the threaded needle to pass through the canvas holes easily, without disturbing canvas threads. The eye of the needle should be large enough to allow yarn to be threaded easily. If the eye is too small, yarn will wear thin and may break.

WORKING WITH PLASTIC CANVAS
Throughout this issue the lines of the canvas will be referred to as threads. However, they are not actually "threads" since the canvas is nonwoven. To cut plastic canvas pieces accurately, count **threads** (not **holes**) as shown in **Fig. 1**.

Fig. 1

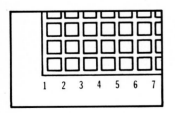

PREPARING AND CUTTING CANVAS
Before cutting out your pieces, notice the thread count of each piece on your chart. The thread count is usually located above the piece on the chart. The thread count tells you the number of threads in the width and height of the canvas pieces. As you can see on our sample chart, the thread count of the Chicken is 18 x 18 threads. Follow the thread count to cut out a rectangle the specified size. Remember to count **threads**, not **holes**. If you accidentally count holes, your piece is going to be the wrong size. Follow the chart to trim the rectangle into the desired shape.

You may want to mark the outline of the piece on your canvas before cutting it out. Use a China marker, grease pencil, or fine point permanent marker to draw the outline of your shape on the canvas. Before you begin stitching, be sure to remove all markings with a dry tissue. Any remaining markings are likely to rub off on your yarn as you stitch.

If there is room around your chart, it may be helpful to use a ruler and pencil to extend the grid lines of the chart to form a rectangle (see Sample Chart).

Sample Chart

Chicken (18 x 18 threads)

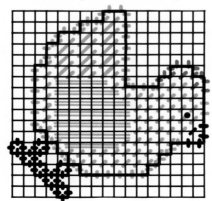

A good pair of household scissors is recommended for cutting plastic canvas. However, a craft knife is helpful when cutting a small area from the center of a larger piece of canvas. For example, a craft knife is recommended for cutting the opening out of a tissue box cover top. When using a craft knife, be sure to protect the table below your canvas. A layer of cardboard or a magazine should provide enough padding to protect your table.

When cutting canvas, be sure to cut as close to the thread as possible without cutting into the thread. If you don't cut close enough, "nubs" or "pickets" will be left on the edge of your canvas. Be sure to cut off all nubs from the canvas before you begin to stitch, because nubs will snag the yarn and are difficult to cover.

When cutting plastic canvas along a diagonal, cut through the center of each intersection. This will leave enough plastic canvas on both sides of the cut so that both pieces of canvas may be used. Diagonal corners will also snag yarn less and be easier to cover.

The charts may show slits in the plastic canvas (**Fig. 2**). To make slits, use a craft knife to cut exactly through the center of an intersection of plastic canvas threads (**Fig. 3**). Repeat for the number of intersections needed. When stitching the piece, be careful not to carry yarn across slits.

Fig. 2

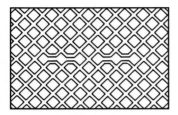

Fig. 3

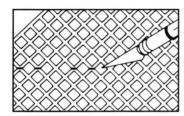

If your project has several pieces, you may want to cut them all out before you begin stitching. Keep your cut pieces in a sealable plastic bag to prevent loss.

THREADING YOUR NEEDLE

Many people wonder, "What is the best way to thread my needle?" Here are a couple of methods. Practice each one with a scrap of yarn and see what works best for you. There are also several yarn size needle threaders available at your local craft store.

FOLD METHOD

First, sharply fold the end of yarn over your needle; then remove needle. Keeping the fold sharp, push the needle onto the yarn (**Fig. 4**).

Fig. 4

THREAD METHOD

Fold a 5" piece of sewing thread in half, forming a loop. Insert loop of thread through the eye of your needle (**Fig. 5**). Insert yarn through the loop and pull the thread back through your needle, pulling yarn through at the same time.

Fig. 5

WASHING INSTRUCTIONS

If you used acrylic yarn for all of your stitches, you may hand wash plastic canvas projects in warm water with a mild detergent. Do not rub or scrub stitches; this will cause the yarn to fuzz. Allow your stitched piece to air dry. Do not put stitched pieces in a clothes dryer. The plastic canvas could melt in the heat of a dryer. Do not dry clean your plastic canvas. The chemicals used in dry cleaning could dissolve the plastic canvas. When piece is dry, you may need to trim the fuzz from your project with a small pair of sharp scissors.

GENERAL INFORMATION

1. **Fig. 1, page 91** shows how to count threads accurately. Follow charts to cut out plastic canvas pieces.
2. Backstitch used for detail (**Fig. 8**) and French Knots (**Fig. 13**) are worked over completed stitches.
3. Overcast Stitch (**Fig. 17, page 94**) is used to cover edges of pieces and to join pieces.

STITCH DIAGRAMS

> Unless otherwise indicated, bring threaded needle up at 1 and all odd numbers and down at 2 and all even numbers.

ALTERNATING MOSAIC STITCH

This three stitch pattern forms small alternating squares as shown in **Fig. 6**.

Fig. 6

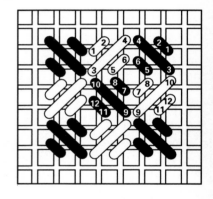

ALTERNATING SCOTCH STITCH

This Scotch Stitch variation is worked over three or more threads, forming alternating blocks (**Fig. 7**).

Fig. 7

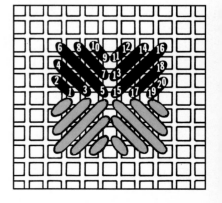

BACKSTITCH

This stitch is worked over completed stitches to outline or define **(Fig. 8)**. It is sometimes worked over more than one thread. Backstitch may also be used to cover canvas as shown in **Fig. 9**.

Fig. 8

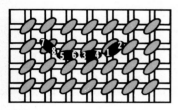

Fig. 9

BEADED TENT STITCH

This stitch is simply a Tent Stitch with a bead slipped on the needle each time before going down at even numbers as shown in **Fig. 10**. Notice that your floss will slant up to the right just like on the chart but the beads will slant in the opposite direction (up to the left).

Fig. 10

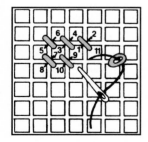

CASHMERE STITCH

This rectangular stitch is formed by working four diagonal stitches as shown in **Fig. 11**.

Fig. 11

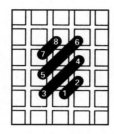

CROSS STITCH

This stitch is composed of two stitches **(Fig. 12)**. The top stitch of each cross must always be made in the same direction.

Fig. 12

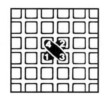

FRENCH KNOT

Bring needle up through hole. Wrap yarn once around needle and insert needle in same hole, holding end of yarn with non-stitching fingers **(Fig. 13)**. Tighten knot; then pull needle through canvas, holding yarn until it must be released.

Fig. 13

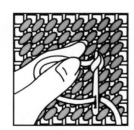

FRINGE

Go down in hole leaving a ¾" end. Holding end in place with thumb, come up in same hole, leaving a 1" loop **(Fig. 14)**. Bring loose end and needle through loop **(Fig. 15)** and pull tightly. Trim strands ⅝" from knot. A dot of glue on back of Fringe will help keep stitches in place.

Fig. 14

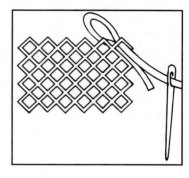

Fig. 15

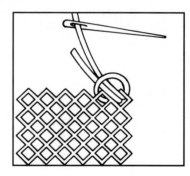

GOBELIN STITCH

This basic straight stitch is worked over two or more threads or intersections. The number of threads or intersections may vary according to the chart **(Fig. 16)**.

Fig. 16

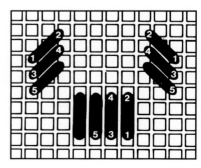

OVERCAST STITCH

This stitch covers the edge of the canvas and joins pieces of canvas (**Fig. 17**). It may be necessary to go through the same hole more than once to get an even coverage on the edge, especially at the corners.

Fig. 17

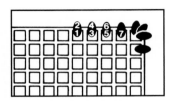

TENT STITCH

This stitch is worked in vertical or horizontal rows over one intersection as shown in **Fig. 18**. Follow **Fig. 19** to work the **Reversed Tent Stitch**.

Fig. 18

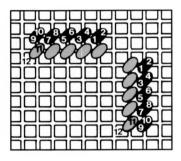

Fig. 19

Sometimes when you are working Tent Stitches, the last stitch on the row will look "pulled" on the front of your piece when you are changing directions. To avoid this problem, leave a loop of yarn on the wrong side of the stitched piece after making the last stitch in the row. When making the first stitch in the next row, run your needle through the loop (**Fig. 20**). Gently pull yarn until all stitches are even.

Fig. 20

TURKEY LOOP STITCH

This stitch is composed of locked loops. Bring needle up through hole and back down through same hole, forming a loop on top of the canvas. A locking stitch is then made across the thread directly below or to either side of loop as shown in **Fig. 21**.

Fig. 21

Instructions tested and photography items made by Janet Akins, Kandi Ashford, Jo Ann Forrest, Kathy Powell, Christel Shelton, Cathy Smith, and Janie Wright.

PROJECT INDEX